The Family Book Of
CAMPING

By LEONARD FABIAN

GALAHAD BOOKS · NEW YORK CITY

TABLE OF CONTENTS

INTRODUCTION

■ For many people the burning question of the century is how to spend their leisure time. This is a problem that becomes almost universal to the citizens of the United States as the growing economy of the country brings more affluence to more and more people.

Camping is the answer for more than 16,000,000 Americans every year and many families make up the bulk of the 16,000,000 campers in America.

From all points of the compass the call of our pioneering heritage radiates its invitation to the mountains, valleys, deserts, forests and seashores and those who are attuned to the siren's song of nature make tracks to the National and State Parks that dot our country like the spots on the face of a kid with freckles.

This book is not just for the beginner but for the experienced woodsman as well. So whether you are a weekender, who reaches his Shangra La with his family via station wagon packed with all the modern conveniences, or an experienced backpacker who makes extended trips into the wilderness with only the barest essentials to brave the elements, you will find in this book information that should answer the questions so often put forth by family campers.

It will cover a broad spectrum of subjects such as shelter, equipment, clothing, cooking, first aid, health, safety and camping skills.

Regardless of the age or size of the reader this book will help him or her find pleasure and learning in outdoor living. ●

CHAPTER ONE

PLANNING

■ Ask any experienced camper about planning a trip and he will, no doubt, tell you that planning, aside from being a necessity, also adds to the pleasure of the trip. Every member of the family takes a part. I knew of one family who actually begin planning their next camping trip the day after returning from a camping trip. The son is in charge of all the equipment—tent, sleeping bags, lanterns, etc. The daughter is in charge of all cooking and eating utensils. The wife is in charge of all correspondence—national and state parks, maps, etc. The father is in charge of tools, axes, knives, packing and transportation.

This does not mean that each member of the family does one job only. It simply designates total responsibility in one area while everyone pitches in and helps in all areas.

Each person has a little notebook into which he jots down ideas and suggestions. One day each week the family sits down and conducts a meeting at which these ideas and suggestions are introduced and discussed. Those ideas and suggestions which are accepted are then written into a master planning book and put into effect the next camping trip.

The abundance of camping areas is probably the main obstacle the camper will find difficult to hurdle. Should he go to the mountains? Desert? Seashore? Great Lakes? Or some out of the way stream in the Catskills? Perhaps a hidden lake in the Rockies? With over 7,000 public camping areas beckoning to you the decision will be hard to make. But once you have made it you must then familiarize yourself with maps of the area. The following list of organizations will be of valuable assistance by supplying you with detailed maps of the camping area you have chosen.

Convenient three-in-one utensil kit.

1. NATIONAL PARK SERVICE, U.S. Department of the Interior, Washington, D.C. 20025. National Parks offer a great many services and facilities besides their lakes and streams which are usually well stocked with fish.

2. FOREST SUPERVISOR, c/o The National Forest, Washington, D.C. 20025. This address is for maps of our national forests.

3. DIRECTOR, Geological Survey, Washington, D.C. 20025. For Topographical maps of areas east of the Mississippi. GEOLOGICAL SURVEY, Federal Center, Denver, Colorado 80215. For topographical maps west of the Mississippi.

Pumpless propane lantern: steady light.

4. COAST & GEODETIC SURVEY, Washington, D.C. 20025. For detailed maps of coastal areas.

5. U.S. LAKE SURVEY OFFICE, 630 Federal Building, Detroit, Michigan 48226. For detailed maps of the Great Lakes.

6. GASOLINE STATIONS have general maps of all the states

Young hiker combination backpack.

which they dispense free of charge.

7. COUNTY COURTHOUSES. Once you have picked your camping area the local county courthouse is an excellent source of supply for maps.

8. Local resorts of commercial camping organizations will supply you with maps free of charge upon your request.

9. NATIONAL CAMPERS AND HIKERS ASSOCIATION, Box 451, Orange, New Jersey 07051 is a clearing house for information given to them by other campers. A written request from you will make them very happy and they will put you in touch with an affiliate organization in your home locale.

10. CHAMBERS OF COMMERCE and tourist boards in every state of the Union have pamphlets, brochures and maps that are available to you free of charge if you will just write for them.

11. "NATIONAL GUIDE TO CAMPGROUNDS AND TRAILER PARKS" is an excellent book that gives detailed information about camps and parks located in every state of the union. Although it does not contain any maps it is a book that we believe every serious camper should have in his library. It sells for $2.98 and it is available at Gulf Service Stations and other outlets.

We mentioned, in the introduction, that there were over 7,000 public camping grounds in the United States. That figure refers to federal campgrounds only. When you combine the state and privately owned camping grounds you wind up with over 15,000 camp grounds in the United States. That figure changes each month as approximately 1,000 new camping grounds are created. Every man, woman and child in this country is living within 100 miles of a campground. This proximity to the campers home base is a convenience when he wants to spend less time traveling and more time basking in the arms of mother nature.

There is a fly in the ointment, however. The average campground accommodates only 100 camp sites, or less. So it is an absolute necessity that you make your reservations far in advance of your planned trip. A typical summer weekend can find an excess of two and a half million campers with only one and a half million camp sites available.

TRAVEL HINTS

For your convenience the following list of agencies should be of assistance when you plan your trip.

ALABAMA: Department of Conservation, Administrative Building, Montgomery, 36104, and the Bureau of Publicity and Information, 304 Dexter Avenue, Montgomery, 36104.

ALASKA: Department of Economic Development and Planning,

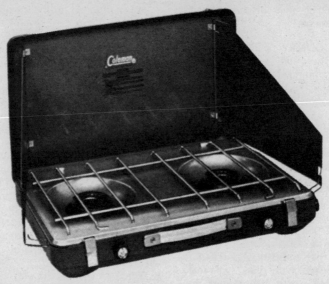

Collapsible, propane camp stove produces up to 10,000 BTUs of controlled heat.

Alaska Travel Division, Juneau, 99801.

ARIZONA: Arizona Development Board, 3443 North Central Avenue, Suite 300, Phoenix, 85012.

ARKANSAS: Arkansas Publicity and Parks Commission, Room 149, State Capitol, Little Rock, 72201.

CALIFORNIA: Department of Parks and Recreation, Division of Beaches and Parks, P.O. Box 2390, Sacramento, 95811.

COLORADO: Department of Public Relations, State Capitol, Denver, 80203.

CONNECTICUT: State Park and Forest Commission, Hartford, 06115, and Connecticut Development Commission, State Office Building, Hartford, 06115.

DELAWARE: State Park Commission, 3300 Faulkland Road, Wilmington, 19808, and Delaware State Development, Tourism Division, 45 The Green, Dover, 19901.

DISTRICT OF COLUMBIA: National Capital Region, 110 Ohio Drive, S.W., Washington, D.C. 20242.

FLORIDA: Florida Park Board, 101 West Gaines Street, Tallahassee, 32304.

GEORGIA: Georgia Department of State Parks, 7 Hunter Street, S.W., Atlanta, 30334.

HAWAII: Hawaii Visitors Bureau, Suite 801, Waikiki Business Plaza, Honolulu, 96815.

IDAHO: Department of Commerce and Development, Room

695, State Capitol Building, Boise, 83701.

ILLINOIS: Department of Conservation, Division of Parks and Memorials, 100 State Office Building, Springfield, 62706.

INDIANA: Department of Natural Resources, 616 State Office Building, Indianapolis, 46204, and Indiana Tourist Assistance Council, State House, Indianapolis, 46204.

IOWA: Public Relations, State Conservation Commission, East 7th and Court, Des Moines, 50308.

KANSAS: Department of Economic Development, State Office Building, Topeka, 66612.

KENTUCKY: Travel Division, Department of Public Information, Capitol Annex Building, Frankfort, 40601.

LOUISIANA: State Parks and Recreation Commission, Old State Capitol Building, P.O. Drawer 111, Baton Rouge, 70821.

MAINE: State Park and Recreation Commission, State House, Augusta, 04330, and Department of Economic Development, State House, Augusta, 04330.

MARYLAND: Department of Forests and Parks, State Office Building, Annapolis, 21404, and Tourist Division, Department of Economic Development, State Office Building, Annapolis, 21404.

MASSACHUSETTS: Department of Natural Resources, 100 Cambridge Street, Boston, 02202, and Massachusetts Department of Commerce, 150 Causeway Street, Boston, 02114.

MICHIGAN: Michigan Tourist Council, Stevens T. Mason Building, Lansing, 48926.

MINNESOTA: Division of State Parks, 320 Centennial Office Building, St. Paul, 55101, and Vacation Information Center, 160 State Office Building, St. Paul, 55101.

MISSISSIPPI: Mississippi Park System, 1104 Woolfolk Building, Jackson, 39201.

MISSOURI: Missouri State Park Board, P.O. Box 176, Jefferson City, 65101, and Division of Commerce and Industrial Development, Travel Recreation Section, Jefferson Building, Jefferson City, 65101.

MONTANA: Advertising Department, Montana Highway Commission, Helena, 59601.

NEBRASKA: Nebraskaland, State Capitol, Lincoln, 68509.

NEVADA: State Park System, Room 221, Nye Building, 201 South Fall Street, Carson City, 89701, and Department of Economic Development, Carson City, 89701.

NEW HAMPSHIRE: Division of Economic Development, State House Annex, Concord, 03301.

NEW JERSEY: Department of Conservation and Economic Development, Forests and Parks Section, P.O. Box 1889, Trenton, 08625, and State Promotion Service, P.O. Box 1889, Trenton, 08625.

NEW MEXICO: State Tourist Division, 302 Galisteo, Santa Fe, 87501, and State Park and Recreation Commission, P.O. Box 1147, Santa Fe, 87501.

NEW YORK: Conservation Department, Division of Lands and Forests, Bureau of Forest Reclamation, State Campus, Albany, 12226; Division of Parks, State Campus, Albany, 12226, and Department of Commerce, Travel Bureau, 112 State Street, Albany, 12207.

NORTH CAROLINA: Travel and Promotion Division, Department of Conservation and Development, Raleigh, 27602.

NORTH DAKOTA: Travel Department, North Dakota State Capitol, Bismarck, 58501.

OHIO: Division of Parks and Recreation, Ohio Department of Natural Resources, 913 Ohio Departments Building, Columbus, 43212, and Development Department Information Center, Room 1007, Ohio Departments Building, Columbus, 43215.

OKLAHOMA: Industrial Development and Park Department, Tourist Information Division, Memorial Building, Oklahoma City, 73105.

OREGON: Travel Information Division, State Highway Department, Salem, 97310.

PENNSYLVANIA: State Department of Forests and Waters, Harrisburg, 17120, and Travel Development Bureau, Department of Commerce, 113 South Office Building, Harrisburg, 17120.

RHODE ISLAND: Division of Parks and Recreation, 83 Park Street, Providence, 02903.

SOUTH CAROLINA: Division of State Parks, Commission of Forestry, P.O. Box 287, Columbia, 29202, and State Development Board, P.O. Box 927, Columbia, 29202.

SOUTH DAKOTA: Publicity Division, Department of Highways, Pierre, 57501.

TENNESSEE: Division of State Parks, 235 Cordell Hull Building, Nashville, 37203, and Division of Information and Tourist Promotion, 264 Cordell Hull Building, Nashville, 37203.

TEXAS: Parks and Wildlife Department, John H. Regan Building, Austin, 78701, and Texas Highway Department, Travel and Information Division, Austin, 78701.

UTAH: Tourist and Publicity Council, Council Hall, Capitol Hill, Salt Lake City, 84114.

VERMONT: Department of Forests and Parks, Montpelier, 05602.

VIRGINIA: Division of Parks, Suite 403, Southern States Building, 7th and Main Streets, Richmond, 23219, and Department of Conservation and Economic Development, 911 Broad Street, Richmond, 23219.

VIRGIN ISLANDS: Virgin Islands National Park, P.O. Box 1707, Charlotte Amalie, St. Thomas, 00801.

WASHINGTON: Visitor Information Bureau, General Administration Building, Olympia, 98501.

WEST VIRGINIA: Division of Parks and Recreation, Department of Natural Resources, State Office

Building, Charleston, 25305, and Department of Commerce, Planning and Research Division, State Capitol Building, Charleston, 25305.

WISCONSIN: Vacation and Travel Service, Conservation Department, P.O. Box 450, Madison, 53701.

WYOMING: Travel Commission, 2320 Capitol Avenue, Cheyenne, 82001.

CANADA

ALBERTA: Alberta Government Travel Bureau, 331 Highways Building, Edmonton.

BRITISH COLUMBIA: British Columbia Government Travel Bureau, Parliament Buildings, Victoria.

MANITOBA: Tourist Development Branch, Department of Industry and Commerce, Winnipeg.

NEW BRUNSWICK: New Brunswick Travel Bureau, 796 Queen Street, Fredericton.

NEWFOUNDLAND: Newfound-land Tourist Development Office, St. John's.

NOVA SCOTIA: Nova Scotia Travel Bureau, Department of Travel and Industry, Halifax.

ONTARIO: Ontario Development of Tourism and Information, Parliament Buildings, Toronto.

PRINCE EDWARD ISLAND: Prince Edward Island Travel Bureau, Box 1987, Charlottetown.

QUEBEC: Department of Tourism, Fish and Game, Parliament Buildings, Quebec City.

SASKATCHEWAN: Tourist Development Branch, Power Building, Regina.

For any additional information, write to the Bureau of Outdoor Recreation, Washington, D.C., 20240 or the National Parks Service, Washington, D.C., 20240, and the Canadian Government Travel Bureau, 150 Kent Street, Ottawa, Ontario. Be sure to include your request for any specific information, hunting, fishing, historic sites, etc., in your letter. •

One of the many attractive areas that bid the camper to stay awhile.

11

CHAPTER TWO

TRANSPORTATION

The jeep; brawny, reliable fun vehicle.

Ease of handling, the hallmark of RVs.

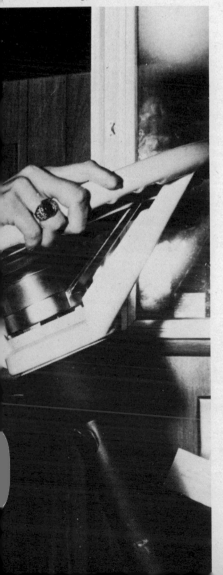

Terra Tiger, 18 hp ATV on land or water.

Mini-trail bikes make the going easy.

13

• The call of the wild is not a hula hoop fad. It is so ingrained in the American people that it can almost be considered peculiar to our culture.

This yearning to return to nature has not gone unheeded by men of imagination and ingenuity. These men have created industries to cater to the needs of the millions of camping buffs in this country and they are finding it rough to keep up with the new developments being urged on them by millions of campers.

The invention of the internal combustion engine and, in turn, the modern highway was definitely a boon for the camper who wanted to get away from the rat race and the camper gave the automobile industry a shot in the arm by demanding specialized vehicles.

There are several things to be considered before you go out and buy that specialized vehicle.

1. Where are you going?
2. How many people must it accommodate?
3. How much money can you afford to spend?

The main consideration for car and trailer camping is the accessibility to the campsite and that means you must have passable roads.

One of the industries created by the camper, specializes in the manufacture of what is now defined as "The Recreational Vehicle." A Recreational Vehicle can be described as portable living accommodations designed for camping and travel. Travel trailers, truck campers, camping trailers and self-powered motor homes are the four categories of Recreational Vehicles manufactured today. These vehicles can be moved from place to place by driving, towing or hauling.

MOBILE HOMES

The cost of a mobile or motor home can range from $4,000.00 to $25,000.00. The $4,000.00 model could be a Volkswagen Bus with 2 bunks, a 2 burner stove and a compact refrigerator. The $25,000.00 model is a palace on wheels. It can sleep four very comfortably. It has a kitchen with a 4 burner stove and an oven, a sink, dish closets, shower, chemical toilet, tables, chairs, sofa, electric or gas lights. In other words, all the comforts of home in one self contained unit with a drivers seat and steering wheel at the front end. Wall to wall carpeting really puts the finishing touch to it all.

The mobile home is not made for the man who wants to rough it. It is for the man who wants to travel but likes to take his comfort with him.

This recreational vehicle cannot go very far off of the paved roads so don't expect to get very far from people when you own one of these babies. For it's size, it manuevers well but it still has to be handled like a greyhound bus.

I believe that the mobile home is for the retired man and his wife who do not want to be tied down to a house in one single community. With a mobile home they can live in Florida during the season and then travel north leisurely during the summer months or even take a cross country trip and

Travel trailers encompass all the necessities and many of the luxuries of home.

The motor home is for those who like "roughing it" in the utmost comfort.

stay in any one place as long as they desire.

It is definitely too heavy an investment for the man who likes to take weekend trips and is limited to a two week vacation just once a year. They are big and beautiful and I know people who are planning to sell their homes when the children have grown so that they can buy a mobile home and travel all over the U.S., Canada and Mexico.

The Travel Trailer or "Pop-Up Convertible" is a very popular Recreational Vehicle. It is compact and lightweight and, depending on the size, can easily be towed behind an economy car.

Measuring about 4 by 7 feet, they do not block rear window vision and there is very little wind-resistance or drag.

When ready for use, four adjustable legs support the body of the trailer and a collapsible frame swings into place to support a large tent which may contain one or two built-in double beds complete with mattresses and bedding plus enough room left over for two cots and several air mattresses.

Another feature of this Travel Trailer is that with all the beds, cots and mattresses there is still plenty of room to store your camping gear, clothes and other accessories. It is also light enough to be manipulated by hand when it has to be rolled to a campsite not accessible by car or for storage. And the Travel Trailer with the hard plastic top can, when not in use, be left out of doors no matter what the season is.

The back pack or piggy back

trailer camper needs to be seated in the bed of a pickup truck. Its size is restricted to the weight limitations and dimensions of the pickup truck. But this does not limit the luxury of space and equipment built into these trailers. The following list is just a sampling of the conveniences you can expect in this recreational vehicle.

1 to 3 single beds
Folding Table
Lights (Butane Gas)
Stove (Butane Gas)
Refrigertor (Butane Gas)
Space Heater (Butane Gas)
Sink
Cupboards
Chemical Toilet (Optional)

Most people who employ the piggy back camper with the pick up rig find it necessary to use the truck for other than camping purposes. This means that the trailer must be removed. This feat is accomplished very easily by the use of a hoist commonly hung from garage beams to facilitate the placement or removal of the trailer from the truck bed.

Many self contained units are manufactured by Ford, General Motors as well as Volkswagen and other manufacturers. These units may contain sleeping accommodations for two or when used in conjunction with the Pop-Up Convertible, it can contain a sink, stove, chemical toilet and storage bins with plenty of room to spare.

A recent innovation by many camping buffs is the conversion of old school busses into self contained recreational vehicles. These converted busses are usually transformed into very comfortable and

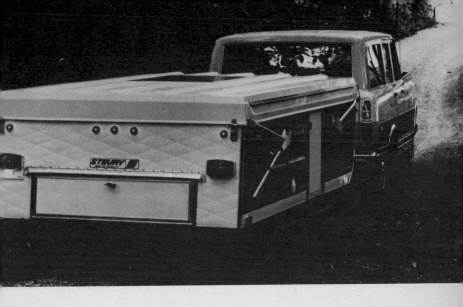

The popular "pop-up convertible" is lightweight and compact, offering little wind resistance when towed. When ready for use it is a comfortable, cozy camper.

17

practical camping vehicles by their owners. They have plenty of sleeping room and, depending on the ability of the individual doing the designing and building, all the conveniences of a very expensive rolling home.

A gentleman in Westbury, Long Island bought a second hand Cadillac hearse that was in excellent condition and with his own labor and ingenuity, a new paint job and some carpeting, turned it into a very attractive recreational vehicle.

The station wagon can be transformed into a camper at very little expense to the owner.

There is the wagon top tent with inner spring, foam or air mattresses that sleeps two. It sits conveniently on top of the car and is accessible by ladder. When not in use it folds down into a package that is only 9 inches high.

You can add many feet of living or sleeping space to a station wagon by using the rear-end canvas extension or boot. Used in conjunction with the wagon top tent, the station wagon is transformed into a complete recreational vehicle.

You can be assured of proper ventilation and security against bugs and insects by purchasing especially designed window screens. These are made for any car and guaranteed to work by the manufacturer.

The station wagon camper used in conjunction with the Pop-up Convertible or the smaller Umbrella tent adds those extra rooms as the camper's family increases.

For the camper who wants to take a great many of the urban comforts along on his trip, there is the deluxe trailer. It's size ranges from 6 by 13 feet to 8 by 30 feet and it can be towed behind your car or station wagon.

For a family consisting of two adults and three children, the recommended size is 8 by 18 feet. Sleeping accommodations consist of double decker bunks. The bottom bunk is a three-quarter size bed and the top is a single bed. Both beds have innerspring, hair or foam rubber mattresses. The dining nook, which seats four, is easily converted into another three-quarter size bed. There is a stove, refrigerator, heater and gas-mantle lamp and they all operate on bottled gas which is carried in tanks attached to the outside of the trailer. (Electric lights can be utilized when camping in an area that supplies electric power.) A 20 gallon water tank supplies the sink and small shower. (The sink and shower can be hooked up to any standard water outlet). There is also a chemical toilet as well as convenient closet space. These trailers have built-in brakes which operate mechanically off of the trailer hitch and stop lights and reflectors.

All camping equipment is not only for sale it is also for rent. There are organizations that specialize in the rental of everything from sleeping bags to the aforementioned deluxe trailer. If you are an individual who is trying to make up his mind about just what kind of recreational vehicle to buy, it is suggested that you rent one before you buy it. No matter

Many desirable features are integral parts of this camper.

Barbecuing and bass fishing are some of the advantages of mobile camping.

how little one spends it is more than depressing to find that the item purchased is unsuitable to ones needs.

When towing a trailer it is wise to drive at reduced speeds. The recommended speed for towing deluxe trailers of any size is 45 miles per hour. Practice backing up and parking until you have mastered the techniques. All turns must be made very wide.

Never leave on a camping trip without first checking out your route. Trailers are not permitted on parkways. This holds true for some turnpikes and most tunnels.

The trailer hitch is a very important part of your camping equipment. Do not settle for second best where a hitch is concerned. You might also find it an added convenience to have a trailer hitch attached to the front of your car. It will facilitate precision trailer parking.

It is suggested that you copy the following list and place it in a conspicuous place in your trailer or behind the sun visor of your car. Anyone going on a camping trip without including every item on this list is going to be caught short in an emergency.

1. Spare tire.
2. Jack.
3. Lug wrench.
4. Tool kit. (Complete)
5. Flasher lights. (Front and rear)
6. Flares.
7. Fire extinguisher.
8. Five gallon can of gasoline. (Well sealed metal can)
9. Two quarts of oil.
10. Spare can of transmission fluid. (For power steering unit)
11. Length of rubber hose. (36 inches. For syphon)
12. Water can or bucket.
13. Funnel. (Metal or plastic)
14. Jumper cables.
15. Extra spark plugs.
16. Extra fan belt.
17. Quick start ignition fluid. (For damp or wet plugs.)
18. Aerosol tire inflator and sealant.
19. Tire cleats or chains.
20. Extra flashlights and batteries.

For further information about trailers or recreational vehicles write to:

RECREATIONAL VEHICLE INSTITUTE, Inc.
2720 Des Plaines Avenue
Des Plaines, Illinois 60018

Tell them how much you have decided you can afford to purchase a recreational vehicle and they will see to it that you receive pamphlets and pertinent information on vehicles within your price range.

For the potential DeLuxe Trailer buyer who is, or through necessity must be, hyper-economy minded, we suggest the used trailer market. You can pick up some excellent buys from campers whose families have outgrown the size of their trailers.

The car-top carrier can more than double the trunk space of the average sedan and it can turn a station wagon into a modern day pack mule.

There are car-top carriers designed specifically for skis, small boats or to carry extra camping gear. Those for camping gear are either enclosed boxes or metal frames covered with zippered canvas.

Most car-top carriers rest on rubber suction cups and are held in place by straps which attach to the rain gutters.

When loading the car-top carrier always place the heaviest loads at the rear.

Car-top carriers can be purchased at any department store that features a sporting goods section. Check your newspapers for special sales. ●

TIPS ON RECREATION VEHICLE SHOWS

With over 800 manufacturers and 10,000 dealers in the country, the recreational vehicle business is Big Business in every way. Any business that generates a volume of over 1.5 billion dollars could hardly be called anything else, according to Jerry Mullaney, a veteran RV show producer.

Mullaney, whose 14 years of credits include assembling the RV shows at New York's Madison Square Garden, makes the following points on the subject of buying a recreational vehicle:

1. Best for serious buyers are single-purpose RV shows, not multi-theme camping shows.

2. Order your camper in January for spring delivery. It normally takes four months from date of purchase.

3. Be sure to check every vehicle in your size and price range before deciding on model. The opportunity to do this is one of the prime reasons for buyers to attend a show in the first place.

This RV is air conditioned by nature.

Interiors are pleasant and efficient.

CHAPTER THREE

THE VANISHING
WILDERNESS

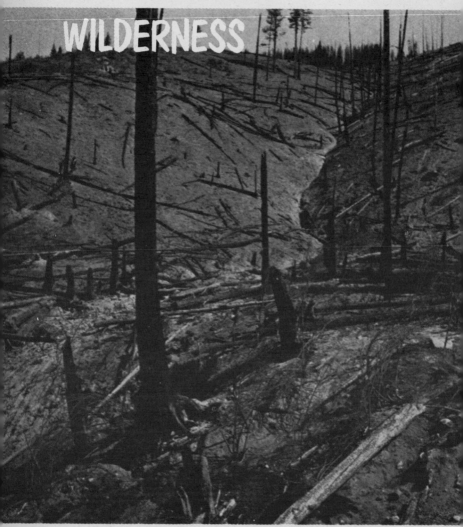

22

■ There is a constant threat to our remaining wilderness areas. Efforts are being made by commercial enterprises to strip our remaining forests or to crack the earth to sap her sources of hidden energy. Regretfully, those people in positions of responsibility don't seem to be able to stem the tide of encroachment into the ever-shrinking wilderness. The people who are interested in protecting these areas are circumvented by various legal maneuvers or indifference on the part of the general public.

You can put a stop to this ravishment of our state and federal parks by joining those organizations that are dedicated to the protection of America's natural beauty. Even if you cannot donate money you can lend your name which might just act as the finger in the dike. You can contact these organizations through literature distributed through camping clubs or advertised in camping periodicals.

There are those who claim that outer space is the new frontier. There are very few who will argue that point. But it will be more than a century before the average man will be able to spend his leisure time camping on some distant planet and even then this adventure will be experienced by a very select minority. Until then, or even then, what can compare to poking the coals of an open camp fire, fishing in a cool clear mountain stream or just relaxing in the natural bosom of the blue-green mountains, hills and valleys of Mother Earth.

WILDERNESS TRAILS IN THE U.S.A.

Of the three million square miles that makes up the land area of the United States there are just 100,000 miles of wilderness trails on Federal and State lands re-

The thoughtful, considerate camper can help stem the tide of encroachment.

served specifically for foot and horseback campers. Automobiles, trailers, motor scooters, bicycles and even snowmobiles are forbidden to enter these areas.

On the east coast the Appalachian Trail is the oldest and best known of the trail systems. Starting at Mt. Katahdin, Maine it wends its way through New Hampshire, Vermont, Massachusetts, Connecticut, New York, New Jersey, Pennsylvania, Maryland, West Virginia, Tennessee, North Carolina ending in Springer Mountain, Georgia.

The trail is accessible from all thirteen of the above mentioned states. You drive to an official parking area and then back pack in for ten or more miles and spend the night, weekend or more, doing what you like to do best.

Complete information as well as detailed guide books may be obtained by writing to the Appalachian Trail Conference, 1718 N. St., N.W., Washington, D.C. 20036.

Starting at the Canadian border in Vermont, the Long Trail continues for 255 miles into Massachusetts. Eighty miles of this beautiful trail are located in Green Mountain National Forest. There are many fine shelters along this well-marked trail. Information is available by writing to the Green Mountain Club, 63 Center Street, Rutland, Vermont.

The Finger Lake Trail is another wilderness area in New York State. It extends from the Catskills to Allegheny State Park. It continues on to the Bruce Trail in Ontario, Canada. The total length of the trail is 650 miles. There are many spur trails that lead to the lakes. Information is available from Mrs. Karby Wade, Finger Lakes Trail, 2783 Brighton-Henrietta Town Line Road, Rochester, N.Y. 14623.

Pennsylvania has two very beautiful trails. Starting at Freeport and running 110 miles north to Cook Forest State Park is the Baker Trail. It is a well marked trail running through farm and woodland and contains 5 shelters. Mail inquiries to the Pittsburgh Council of American Youth Hostels, 6300 Fifth Avenue, Pittsburgh, Pa. 15232.

Pennsylvania's other trail is the Horse-Shoe Trail. It is 121 miles long. It begins at Valley Forge and ends in Rattling Run on Sharp Mountain. Sharp Mountain is 12 miles north of Hershey, Pa. You can pack into this trail on horseback. For information write to Mr. W.N. West III, President, Horse-Shoe Trail Club, 1600 Three Penn Center Plaza, Philadalphia, Pa. 19102.

The Florida Trail may, or may not, be completed by the time this book reaches publication. Information may be obtained by writing to the Florida Trail Assn., 33 S.W. 18th Terrace, Miami, Fla. 33129.

Ohio's 150 mile Buckeye Trail is to be extended across all of southern Ohio and north to Lake Erie. Complete information available from the Buckeye Trail Assn., Box 758, Logan, Ohio 43138.

The state of Michigan has a Shore to Shore Trail. It is 200 miles long and runs from Lake Michigan to Lake Huron. Detailed information may be obtained from the Michigan Department of Conservation, Lansing, Mich. 48926.

On the Pacific Coast we have the Pacific Crest Trail that extends from Canada to Mexico— 2,000 miles of foot trail, this is a back-packers dream. Pack horses and burros are permitted on this trail. You can start out in the Cascade Mountains in Washington, move on down through Oregon and then into the Sierra Nevada Mountains in California and wind up with the last 400 miles of your trip in the desert. The Pacific Crest Trail System Conference, Hotel Green, Pasadena, California will send complete information upon request.

We suggest that if you wish to visit any of these wilderness areas that you write for maps and rules and regulations of the park. Be sure to register with the park rangers and inform them of the length of time you expect to stay in the park. This is for your safety. ●

Tracts of land must remain "forever wild" as a heritage for future generations.

CHAPTER FOUR

CHOOSING YOUR CAMPSITE

■ The choice of a campsite can make the difference in a successful or unsuccessful camp-out. The novice who attempts an overnight camping trip without first learning the basics of where to set up his camp is not only asking for a disappointing trip but, in some instances, possible tragedy. The following dos and don'ts should be copied and carried along on all camping trips by novices as well as experienced campers.

1. The campsite must be located early enough in the afternoon to take advantage of the available sunlight so that all setting up is completed before darkness.

2. Use your compass to locate due east. Then set up your camp so that all campsite activities have the best natural light during the daylight hours.

3. A prime requisite of any successful campsite is water and wood. The lack of either one, or both of these necessities can ruin a camp-out before it gets started.

4. An area no less than twice the size of your tent and vehicle must be cleared of stones, twigs, branches and sticks. This double area will give you the room necessary for cooking, fireplace, table, storage and elbow room. The removal of stones, twigs, etc., prevents damage to canvas tent bottoms, tires, as well as preventing twisted ankles or broken bones.

5. The weather is an important factor that must be considered when setting up your camp. Even though the weatherman predicts fair weather you must remember that they are not 100% accurate. Therefore, you must set up your camp as though you were expecting a cloud burst. This is not as difficult as it sounds. Just don't set up your camp in any hollow or gully that might fill up with water or turn muddy.

6. Do not set your camp up any closer than thirty feet to any stream, lake or river. There are several reasons for this advice. Cold air settles at lower levels as well as dampness and fog. The insects are in such abundance at night around water that they can almost drive you crazy. The last and most im-portant reason is the resultant tragedy that could occur if there is a sudden rain storm up-stream and a flash flood should take place while you are asleep in your tent.

7. At all times, avoid setting up camp in tall grass. This rule stands for the seashore as well as the mountains. Tall grass contains ticks, chiggers, mosquitos and possibly deadly snakes.

8. To be comfortable when camping during the hot summer months it is necessary to pitch your tent under trees that will over-shade and protect you from the sun. First check the trees for rotting or dead branches that could break off in a stiff breeze and damage your equipment. ●

In choosing a campsite, follow the rules that will make your trip more pleasant.

CHAPTER FIVE

HIKING AND THE HUMAN CARRIER

How many times have you heard someone make the statement, "Backpack hiking is for the birds. I tried it once and I thought I would collapse before we had gone a mile." We agree that backpacking can sometimes be a hot and sweaty job. But there is no reason for it to be pure torture. Overloading and poor ventilation between the pack and the carriers back can put the strongest man to bed with all kinds of complaints for more than a week. A pack that allows air to circulate between the pack and your back will help to eliminate much of your discomfort.

Oversize Canadian pack, for portaging.

The mountain climbers rucksack is a good example of what I am talking about. It is a broad-bottomed, waterproof canvas bag with several pockets. The frame is made of lightweight tubular steel and it curves out from the body which helps it to support the pack. A waist-high webbed strap is the only thing that touches the body. The smaller rucksack without a frame is recommended for one day outings. It will carry the necessary food and extra sweater to ward off the chill when you hike back that night.

The Duluth pack has shoulder straps and a tumpline. A tumpline

Frame design used on Mt. Everest climb.

29

is a head strap which fits around the forehead which lets the strong neck muscles take on some of the burden. This pack is designed to carry heavy loads for short distances. It is more of a storage pack used for canoe trips.

For carrying tools, canned goods or any of those materials which might dig into the backpackers back, the Adirondack pack basket is recommended. It is made of interwoven ash or willow strips and makes an excellent storage box in camp.

The frame pack is styled for comfort.

The packboard or Everest pack is probably the most versatile backpack of them all. The frame consists of aluminum tubing, leather shoulder straps, plus a web strap that crosses the small of the back. It has a shelf at the bottom that supports the load. It is very lightweight and you don't have to be too particular about the shape and size of the load. Because they are so simple to construct, many campers make their own packboards. The frame consists of 1 by 2 inch pipe; verticles are 30 inches long, 15 inches for the horizontals. Use countersunk brass wood screws to assemble. Use two three inch web bands, one at the shoulder and one at the waist. Lace them tightly. The shoulder straps are one length of 2-inch webbing that tapers to 1-inch so as to pass through the buckles and snaps. Screws and washers secure the strap to the horizontal. Supporting the load at the top is a piece of Masonite.

The rule for loading is the same for all back-packs. Concentrate the weight on your shoulders by packing the heavier items near the top. But do not make the pack top heavy as it can upset your balance. With camping equipment made of such lightweight materials it is possible for a man and his wife to go on a weekend hike packing less than 28 pounds between them. This includes the tent, sleeping bags, cooking utensils and food. With a youngster along toting a small backpack, which always makes him feel like Kit Carson, 3 to 5 pounds can be taken out of Mom and Dad's pack. ●

CHAPTER SIX

MAKING CAMP

Use of basic skills, combined with common sense, help toward making a good camp.

TENTS

■ Camping today is so popular and manufacturers are placing so many tents on the market that one might find it difficult to make a choice as to just which tent to buy. They come in all sizes, shapes and colors and a good salesman could, in his eagerness to make a sale, talk you into buying a tent that is either too small or too large for your needs. He may try to sell you one large tent when it might be more practical for you to have one small tent and one medium sized tent or just two small tents. You are the one who must know what your needs are before you attempt to make your purchase.

How do you go about making this decision? First you must know how many people are going to sleep inside the tent. You must allow 4 by 8 feet for each person. This figure has been computed for sleeping bags only. If you use cots it is best to set them up in your living room along with all the other gear that you will take along that is going to take up floor space in your tent. Measure the area and then you will know how much floor space your tent must have in order to be comfortable. These measurements tell you what your needs are for sleeping. What happens if it rains and everyone has to stay inside. Will you be so close to one another that nerves will begin to fray? This is why we mentioned two medium sized or two small tents rather than one large one. You must also take into consideration that a tent with sloping sides gives you less floor space.

Basic umbrella tent: a favorite style.

Umbrella tent with canopy added.

Cottage tent with interior ridgepole.

This cottage tent has large windows.

How long are you going to stay at the campsite? If you are going to camp out for a week or more then the large tent with poles and guy ropes will pose no problem. But if you are only going out for one night or you intend to change your campsite several times over an extended period then you need a tent that can be erected with a minimum of trouble and that is the umbrella tent.

Don't forget to consider cross ventilation when you buy your tent. Make sure that the windows can be covered from the inside. Doorway netting should have complete zipper closings. All points of stress, the ridge and corners, should have reinforcement strips. Pay particular attention to the grommets (metal-rimmed rope holes) and tent-peg loops. For extra strength, all seams should be double overlapped. This means four thicknesses. Wet weather shrinks a tent while dry weather expands it.

The lodgepole tent is similar to, only smaller in design than the fireside tent.

That is why you must look for the above features so that the tent will be able to take the strain.

The best tent material is the lightweight Palina cloth or poplin. Army duck, twill or dry jean are not recommended. Most good tents are waterproofed to last a minimum of five years. After that they can be retreated.

Our only criticism of brightly colored tents is that they get dirty very quickly.

You don't have to take a survey of all the retail sporting goods establishments in order to find out just which tent is the most popular model with campers in the United States. All you have to do is to go to any camping ground and you will see that it is the umbrella tent. It is quick and simple to set up and it doesn't have any guy ropes to trip over. Its size ranges from 8 to 12 square feet with a built-in floor. The built-in floor is optional.

The tent can be erected in less than 20 minutes. First the floor is staked out and then the frame is popped up from the inside in the same manner in which you would open up an umbrella. The 9 by 11 foot corner post umbrella will comfortably accommodate three adults sleeping on cots and still leave plenty of space for dressing and storage. Using two cots and two sleeping bags it will accommodate four adults.

The center pole, which has often been considered a nuisance, can perform another function besides holding up the tent. The upper portion of the center pole, about eye level, can be fitted with a portable shelf. The shelf can

hold a mirror, lantern, flashlight or whatever else you might think of. A folding table can also be fitted around the center pole. To make the shelf you first cut a board to the size to suit your convenience. Then drill a hole in the center of the board that is the circumference of the center pole. Cut the board in half and attach a V-bracket to each half with wood screws. Take the two halves and fit them around the center pole. The shelf is now secured to the center pole by using one or two hose clamps.

A similar arrangement can be used to set up your table on the center pole. The addition of folding legs or removable legs will assist in supporting the table. The area under the table can be utilized as storage space.

Do not try to sleep more than four people in a tent unless the one or two extra persons happen to be very young children. If you find that you need a tent that will accommodate from six to eight people then we suggest that you buy two medium sized tents rather than one big one. You will also find that two medium sized tents are easier to keep neat and easier to store and carry.

When buying a new tent there is no need to be concerned about directions on how to set the tent up as the manufacturer sees that directions are included with each tent that leaves the factory. If you are taking our advice and renting a tent before purchasing one, then you must be explicit in your request to the salesman about receiving the directions. The person who had rented the tent previously may have inadvertantly misplaced them. You may also want to practice setting up your tent in your back yard or, if you are an apartment dweller, on your roof or in your living room. It is a good idea to get the feel of how the tent sets up before you go on your camping trip.

Be sure to re-read the section Choosing Your Campsite before you leave on your trip.

CAMPFIRES

To some campers the end of a perfect day in the wilderness is sitting around a campfire having a bull session with the boys or if it is a family outing the bull session becomes ghost stories with the kids. If the kids happen to be in their teens, the campfire seems to loosen up their tongues and the generation gap goes up in the flames.

Starting a fire is relatively simple. Paper is available from food containers and with a few small twigs on top of that to act as kindling your logs should burn without very much trouble. Then there are the commercial fire starters, both solid and liquid that can be transported without taking up too much space.

Many of the supermarkets are selling logs that burn in various colors. You can achieve the same effect without spending any extra money. For a blue-green effect you can sprinkle some copper chloride on the fire. Copper metal fillings added to some copper ammonium chloride will add some other hues to the blaze or just copper metal fillings by themselves. The same colorful effect

can be achieved using natural wood in the following combinations. Oak, pine and birch. The oak will give you heat, the pine will give you scent and the birch will add the color. Hemlock and spruce can be substituted for the pine and ash and maple can be substituted for the birch. Oak is necessary for the slow hot burn.

You can't have a good fire without a good axe or hatchet. Knowing how to use one is the sign of a good outdoorsman. Yet, even a good woodsman can have an accident if he tries to take a

The campfire mystique is difficult to explain but wonderful to experience.

short cut when he is in a hurry. Be aware of the following basic rules and avoid unnecessary problems.

1. Never remove sheath or cover until ready for use. (Same rule applies to knives.)

2. Always wipe metal with oil or bacon grease for rust prevention. (This rule is also applicable to knives.)

3. DO NOT attempt to split a round log by hitting it on the side in a lengthwise position.

4. DO NOT attempt to split a log on the ground.

5. DO NOT attempt to split a log on a flat stone.

6. DO NOT attempt to cut logs or sticks on any uneven surface.

7. DO place log in an upright position on a tree stump.

8. DO strike log on top only.

9. DO NOT hold log or allow anyone else to hold log when cutting is taking place.

10. DO NOT try to hold log with your foot.

Smaller sticks should never be chopped with an axe or a hatchet. Break them with your hands or hand and foot pressure.

Many of the Federal, State and commercial campgrounds provide ready-made fireplaces at their campsites. They run the gamut in construction from fancy masonry to rugged but very functional rock-piles. These fireplaces have been constructed with safety in mind but fire is fire and there is always the chance of a sudden gust of wind that can start a conflagration that not only destroys the campsite but the surrounding wilderness area.

When setting up your camp consider the prevailing wind and set up your tent so that smoke does not blow inside or a stray spark cannot precipitate a tragedy.

Many camping areas, even those that supply ready-made fireplaces, forbid wood fires. That is because there is a shortage of wood and they are trying to preserve whatever forest is left. It is therefore necessary for you to carry along a supply of charcoal briquets. A ten or twenty pound bag of charcoal may not be a burden for the vehicular camper but it is definitely out of the question for the hiking backpacker. He will have to rely on the small portable stove with canned heat or sterno.

Although a charcoal fire throws off plenty of heat it can be augmented by laying the charcoal briquets evenly on some heavy foil. The foil acts as a reflector and it also aids in cleaning up when the fire is out.

The following four methods of fire building are just suggestions. Pick the method that suits your requirements.

1. *TEPEE:* Stack wood on end in a circle and lean the tops so that they touch. The tepee can be enjoyed from all sides.

2. *CRISSCROSS:* To insure ventilation build this one on two larger logs or long rocks.

3. *REFLECTOR:* Several logs stacked on top of one another, similar to a lean-to, with rocks supporting the back. This throws the heat of the fire outward.

4. *TRENCH:* Dig a trench deep enough to hold your fire. Then lay some oak branches or pipes across the trench to support your cooking utensils.

Watch your children very carefully when they are around the fire. Charcoal fires can fool you. They may appear to be burned out but they can still be very much alive. Drown all fires! Do not spare the water when dousing your fire.

OUTDOOR COOKING

Modern technology has certainly improved the campers diet. Pre-packaged foods, new methods for preserving foods along with instant mixes and other dehydrated staples have given the camper something to look forward to besides the old stand-by of bacon, beans and coffee.

With such a wide variety of foods to choose from we are not going to attempt to tell you what to take along with you. You know just how much room you have in your camper or how much you can carry in a backpack. We will only list those items that are considered as basics and it is up to you to decide which are essential for your trip.

1. Butter—margarine.
2. Bread—rolls—crackers.
3. Coffee, powdered—pre-packaged perk.
4. Cocoa—powdered or block. Chocolate drink—powdered.
5. Orange juice, Grapefruit juice, Twang. Frozen—Powdered.
6. Salt, Pepper, Monosodium glutamate.
7. Sugar—sugar substitute—maple syrup.
8. Jelly—jam—preserves.
9. Canned milk—powdered milk.
10. Pancake or buckwheat flour.
11. Catsup—barbecue sauce—Worcestershire sauce.
12. Instant rice.
13. Spaghetti—Noodles—Canned or boxed.
14. Cheese (Many varieties.)
15. Peanut butter.
16. Eggs (See suggestion at end of this list)
17. Ham—Spam—Hot dogs—canned.
18. Hash—canned.
19. Bacon—Canadian bacon.
20. Dried chipped beef—canned.
21. Kraft dinner—packaged.
22. Vegetables—canned.
23. Tomatoes—tomato paste—canned.
24. Onions—fresh—canned—dried.
25. Chicken—pre-cooked—canned.
26. Salmon—tuna fish—canned.
27. Herring—Sardines—smoked—canned.
28. Pork and beans—canned.
29. Potatoes—fresh—canned—instant powdered.

Pre-sliced bacon may be a convenience but it is much easier to preserve a side of bacon. To avoid molding and to keep the bacon fresh, wash it off with a clean cloth using vinegar instead of water. The vinegar also helps to keep the bacon fresh tasting.

After frying the bacon do not throw away the fat. Pour it into a can or a jar as it can be of further assistance for frying, baking or as a flavoring for lentil or bean or pea soups. Bacon grease can also be used to prevent knives, hatchets and axes from rusting.

Unless you have a deluxe camper with a refrigerator it is almost impossible to take along fresh eggs. But bacon and eggs taste great when cooked out-of-doors. You can have as many fresh eggs as you want if you will break them into a jar before going on your camping trip. Fill the bottle right to the top. The eggs will stay separated and you can pour them out of the jar one at a time as you need them. Be sure to keep them in a cool place when you are not going to use them.

Hard boiled eggs have many uses besides a quick snack for those ever-hungry kids. You can slice them into a salad or use them on a sandwich. Just chill them before you leave home.

Whether cooking at home or at a campsite you should never pour away the vegetable juice. Cook the vegetables in the same juice that comes in the can. It will only add to their flavor. Whatever juice is left over in the pot after cooking should be saved. Combine these vegetable juices and you will come up with a delicious soup. Naturally you can add some greens and carrots as well as potatoes with some chunks of meat to jazz up the flavor. Don't neglect

Food prepared over a campfire is unparalleled in flavor.

to save the juice of any potatoes you might have boiled. The following recipe would satisfy the palate of the most particular gourmet. Take 1 quart of boiled potatoe juice and add some mashed leftover potatoes. Chop up two small onions along with some salt, pepper and dried parsley flakes. Drop in a beef bouillon cube and 4 tablespoons of powdered milk. For added flavor include any leftover vegetable juices. DO NOT INCLUDE THE JUICE OF CABBAGE OR ANY MEMBER OF THE CABBAGE FAMILY. Boil the above ingredients for appoximately 30 to 40 minutes and you will serve up a concoction that will be talked about months after the camping trip is over.

With all the modern equipment available for campers, cooking is no longer the great chore it once was. But just in case you did not take along that dutch or reflector oven here is a suggestion how to bake up some potatoes.

You need a large tin can with a wire handle. The can should be large enough to hold the amount of potatoes you intend to cook or you can use two or more small cans. Holes can be punched in the sides of the can to accommodate the wire handle. Scrub the potatoes well and wrap them individually in some aluminum foil. Place a layer of dirt or sand in the bottom of the can. Now put in your potatoes. Place some more sand or dirt in the can and make sure that each potato has a layer of dirt or sand between them. They must not be touching one another or the sides of the can. Now cover the potatoes completely with your sand or dirt. Add water to the sand until it develops a doughy texture. DO NOT SOAK OR DROWN! Place the can or cans directly into the hot coals piling them high around all sides of the can. Depending on the size of the potatoes, they should be cooked in about an hour. As the dirt or sand dries out keep adding water and make sure that the coals are raked around the cans so that the heat remains constant. To be sure that the potatoes are well baked you can test the top potato in the can. If that one is done they are all done.

When starting out on a camping trip it is best to have breakfast at home before starting. It is doubtful that you will arrive at your destination before lunch time so it is best to have lunch prepared so that you can stop at some roadside picnic area and eat with a minimum of trouble. Sandwiches are your best bet for the roadside lunch. They can be kept fresh in a modern picnic basket

A boon to the camp gourmet is the availability of great, freeze-dry foods.

with some Scotch Ice or ice cubes. Be sure to include some fresh tomatoes along with some hard-boiled eggs. The picnic basket can also hold some canned soda for the kids or perhaps some ice water which can be mixed with some Kool-Aid or other powdered concoction. Mom and Dad can have a thermos of hot coffee or tea.

Once you have arrived at your destination the most immediate need is to set up the camp. Even though everyone has pitched in to make the job easier it is still a chore and no one likes to follow a chore with a chore and after setting up a camp, cooking can be a chore. For this meal we would suggest some pre-boiled chicken. This can be prepared at home the day before the trip or they can be purchased at those stores specializing in this product. The chicken can be served cold or it can be wrapped in aluminum foil and heated on a spit over the fire. Some red beets right out of the can along with some pickles should be very satisfying and it can all be topped off with some canned fruit for dessert.

Another very quick way to prepare a convenient dinner is the pre-packaged pot pie or T.V. Dinner which can be kept cold in the aforementioned picnic basket and cooked over the open fire.

CAMP COOKING WITH EASE

Ask any camper what the greatest invention of the century is and he will no doubt answer "Tin Foil." Actually it is aluminum foil and even though it is not the greatest invention of the century, it certainly is one of the most important items where camp cooking is concerned. You can bake, broil or fry with it. Use it for steaks, fish, poultry, roasts or vegetable. It molds to the shape of whatever food you wrap in it and it retains all the natural flavor of the food. It is a great time saver since it eliminates the use of pots and pans and dishes. That means no dishwashing after cooking and eating.

It also means that all foods can be prepared for cooking before embarking on the camping trip. Since the meats will be kept in a cooler it is possible to pre-season them before wrapping them in your foil. Before wrapping your meat spread some oil, margarine, butter or bacon grease over the meat. Add some salt or pepper or garlic or onion salt.

Fresh vegetables should be sliced and seasoned before wrapping. Vegetables take longer to cook than meat, that is why it is suggested that carrots, onions, etc. be sliced into very small pieces. When ready to cook, the foil wrap should be opened and a tablespoon full of water should be added to prevent the vegetables from burning and sticking to the foil.

Corn on the cob can be salted and buttered before being wrapped in foil.

You will always know what type of food is in the foil if you tag it with a piece of paper and place a rubber band around it. The rubber band should be removed when the food goes on the fire.

Foil wrapped foods can be cooked on grates over a hard

wood or charcoal fire. They can also be layed directly on top of the coals or they can be buried in the coals so that they cook evenly on all sides at the same time.

The food can be eaten directly from the foil. The foil packages can be removed from the fire by using a pair of heavy asbestos gloves, a small shovel or a pair of water-hose pliers.

After allowing a minute or two for the heat of the coals to penetrate the foil, the following times should be adequate for the foods mentioned.

Breads, rolls and biscuits all come in pre-mixed dough so that it isn't necessary to cart along fresh bread which might become stale or moldy. Some of them come already wrapped in foil so that all you have to do is place them in the fire. The choices in breads are varied so that you can take along several of your favorites. Besides white and rye there is whole wheat, onion and garlic. Our family never worries about calories on a camping trip. With all the wood chopping and hiking to be done we burn up more than we consume.

STOVES

Some camping areas do not allow wood fires. This presents a problem for the camper who plans an extensive stay. How is he going to prepare his food? The small portable charcoal grill, or Hibachi, is the answer for some campers. The most popular stove, though, is the two-burner gasoline burning stove. This model sells more than all the other camping stoves combined. It is compact, lightweight and economical to buy and to use. It weighs about 17 pounds and has 12 by 18 inches of working area. The three-burner model weighs 25 pounds with a working area measuring 14 by 25 inches. Since two two-burner models take up the same space as one three-burner model and gives you almost twice the working area, it seems wiser to take two two-burner models on your camping trip. They fold up and close like small metal overnight cases with a handle for convenient carrying and they don't take up too much room in a trailer or station wagon. The model with the folding legs is preferred as it can then be used safely on the back of a station

15 to 20 minutes .... medium sized hamburgers.
15 to 20 minutes .... medium rare steak.
25 to 30 minutes .... poultry quarters.
25 to 30 minutes .... lamb chops. (1 to 1½ inches thick)
30 to 40 minutes .... pork chops. (1 to 1½ inches thick)
60 to 70 minutes .... poultry. (5 lbs. uncut)
70 to 80 minutes .... roast. (medium sized)
100 to 120 minutes .... roast. (large sized)
15 to 20 minutes .... most fish. (time depends on size)
Allow 2 minutes per pound for freshwater fish.

The propane gas stove is extremely efficient and most convenient to use.

that will fit your stove while you are on the road or at the campgrounds. The propane gas stove is not as economical to operate as the gasoline stove.

WARNING!   WARNING!

WARNING! Never throw any gas containers into a fire. Even if they are empty. This is tantamount to committing suicide and mass murder. The propane container will explode like a hand grenade sending shrapnel flying in all directions. If there are wastecan facilities in the campgrounds dispose of them there. If not, bury them in a deep hole with the rest of your nonburnable refuse.

wagon, picnic table or on the ground. The lid, as well as a pair of flaps, shield the stove burners from the wind. An optional piece of equipment is the solid or collapsible oven which comes in handy for baking. When used, it sits right on top of the burners.

The amount of gasoline consumed when cooking on this type of stove is merely one-half pint per burner hour. This is very inexpensive when you consider it only takes 3 minutes to boil up 1 quart of water for a delicious pot of coffee. Fuel is no problem since you can always syphon some gas out of the automobile tank in case of an emergency.

The liquid petroleum or propane gas stoves are a little more convenient to use than the gasoline burner but you must always be sure that your fuel tanks are full and you must carry extras in case you run out. There is no guarantee that you will be able to refill these tanks or buy new ones

COOLERS

If you do not have a trailer that contains an electric or gas operated refrigerator then you must have a portable cooler to help you preserve your food. In a previous section we mentioned the plastic picnic basket or hamper. To be more specific the cooler made out of urethane foam gives the best insulation for cooling. You can get metal coolers that use urethane foam for insulation or the cooler that is all urethane foam. These coolers come in various shapes and sizes but the square shaped cooler measuring 12" by 16" by 22" is recommended for its roominess and packing convenience. Whichever unit you buy, metal covered plastic or all plastic, you will receive excellent results if you pre-cool the hamper in a deep freezer, leaving the cover off, for approximately 12 hours.

Take 4 or 5 plastic juice or milk cartons and fill them with water and freeze them into solid ice. These will be placed in your cooler as you pack your food. There are several commercial products on the market that can be frozen for long lasting cooling effects. Scotch Ice is just one of them.

If you intend to use ice cubes in a plastic bag we suggest that you place them in double paper bags. This will give you better insulation.

Pre-freeze all perishable foods before packing them in the cooler.

Maximum results can be obtained from the cooler in camp if it is kept covered with a wet cloth.

PURE WATER

Play it safe no matter what anyone tells you. It is recommended that you do not drink water from any well, brook, stream, pond or any other source in any isolated area unless you are in a state or federal park where there is a sign clearly indicating that the water is fit for human consumption. Be sure that every member of your camping party is made aware of this cardinal rule. The results cannot only be painful but tragic when this rule is abused. Do not cook in this water either.

Plastic water jugs can be filled before leaving on a camping trip or the commercially filled plastic cartons of water may be purchased at your nearby super market. If carting your water with you is going to cause too great an inconvenience then your best bet is a water purifying kit. The OGDEN FILTER COMPANY OF LOS ANGELES, CALIFORNIA, manufactures a kit and markets it under the name of AQUA-PAC. It purifies, disinfects and filters the water making it safe for drinking and cooking. It achieves this in one simple operation. It is light weight and compact and well worth the $20.00 investment.

Listed below are some other methods for purifying water.

1. Boil water no less than 20 minutes. If water is murky boil it for 40 minutes.

2. Halazone tablets. Two tablets per quart of water and allow 30 minutes for them to disolve and do the job.

3. Iodine Water Purification Tablets. 1 tablet for each quart of water. 2 tablets if water is murky.

4. Liquid Iodine. 2% iodine per quart of water. (Tablets are preferable.)

5. Charcoal. Three or four pieces of charcoal removed from the campfire and dropped into a pot of water. Allow to boil for thirty minutes. Then pour into a container using a clean cloth as a strainer.

6. Filter water by pouring it through a bag of sand and then boil it for 30 minutes.

The preceding methods of water purification will not make the water taste good. They will only make the water safer to drink. ●

PRECAUTIONS AND SAFETY PROCEDURES

PLANTS TO AVOID

■ How many camping trips have been ruined by the introduction of poisonous plants? They would be impossible to count. It is inexcusable when a camper allows himself to come into contact with poison ivy, poison sumac or poison oak as they are easily identifiable. Poison ivy and poison oak, (Poison oak is not related to the oak tree at all. It is just another form of poison ivy.), can be recognized. They have three glossy wax-like leaves on one stem. The underside of their leaves is of a lighter hue. When the plant is young, in the spring, the leaf has a shiny reddish tinge which becomes a glossy green in the summer and then takes on the original reddish tinge in the autumn. It does not loose it's potency during the winter months. These poisonous plants will grow among hedgerows, along fences, among shrubs or even climb poles and trees.

Any area that these plants touch and even the surrounding areas should be considered contaminated. The toxic agent in these plants rubs off on anything they touch and it can be spread by rain.

For some people the infection caused by the toxic agent of these plants causes a minor irritation to those parts of their bodies that have been contaminated. The skin will break out in a rash and a very annoying itch will accompany this rash. Once this has occured medical attention is needed. Preliminary treatment usually recommended is the coating of the infected area with calomine lotion or applying vitamin E. Hands should be washed with soap and water at regular intervals and they should be kept away from the face particularly the eyes and ears.

Poison sumac has been known to grow as high as 20 feet but it can also grow as a small tree or even a bush.

The only member of your camping party who can be immune to poison ivy is your dog, if he happens to be along. He may be immune but he can act as a carrier. If he brushes up against the plant the oil of the plant will rub off on his coat. When you pet him you will become infected. If you have driven over a patch of poison ivy and then get a flat tire you will become infected when you change the tire.

If you or any of your party come in contact with these poisonous plants and you are aware of it you can wash those areas that came in contact with the plant and quite possibly avoid the consequences.

A most important rule to remember is NEVER BURN POISON IVY, OAK OR SUMAC! The smoke from these burning plants is more potent than actual contact with the plant itself. You can also infect unsuspecting nearby campers.

Contact with any of these plants should not be taken lightly. One season you may be able to sleep right on top of them and not be bothered. The next season you may be standing as much as a quarter of a mile away from the plant and the wind will seem to carry the infection to you.

Do not take any infection from these poison plants lightly. What may have only developed into some minor skin eruptions and irritations in the past could without warning develop into a severe allergy that could prove to be fatal.

The other poisonous plants such as mushrooms and berries are too numerous to mention. You should impress the other members of your party with the dangers involved in eating anything except that which has been prepared by the camp cook. With all the thousands of plants that grow on this planet there are only a few hundred that can be eaten in safety by human beings. Eating berries or mushrooms can not only cause serious and painful illness but death itself.

POISONOUS REPTILES

Every year thousands of non-poisonous snakes are killed by un-knowledgeable campers. This is a tragedy because these snakes are very beneficial to mankind. Even the poisonous snake should be allowed to live out his life without interference from man because he too has a definite function to perform in natures scheme. Poisonous as well as non-poisonous snakes destroy rodents and insects which damage crops and spread disease among men. Yet a man will go out of his way to destroy a snake even when the snake is trying to get out of the mans way.

On this entire earth there are only 2,500 different species of snakes. There are only 55 different species in the United States. Of the 55 species in this country only 4 of them are poisonous.

The snake with the widest distribution in the U.S. is the rattlesnake. There are more than a dozen varieties of rattlesnake

There are many kinds of rattlesnakes, but don't always rely on a cicada-like sound to warn you of the presence of one of these highly venomous reptiles.

which are distinguished only by the size they reach at maturity. There is the pygmy rattler whose total length at muturity is just under 1 foot long and various other species which grow longer. The largest of the rattlers is the diamondback which can exceed 7 feet in length at maturity.

All rattlesnakes have one distinguishing characteristic and that is the series of loose, horny segments of buttons at their tail ends which they will usually vibrate or rattle when a trespasser enters their area. Do not depend on this warning rattle as the snake may lose these rattles when molting or they can break off due to strenuous activity on the snake's part. You may come along and the snake may be vibrating his tail section but there is nothing there to vibrate.

In most instances the snake will try to avoid your presence by sneaking away without even letting you know it was there. The snake will not attack you unless it feels that it is threatened and if it is trying to get away and you follow it that will be interpreted by the snake as a threat.

The copperhead ranges from Massachusetts to Texas and although its venom is not considered to be as potent as the rattlesnake's it is still a good idea to treat him with respect. The overall coloring of the copperhead is a copper red with mottled markings that vary in shape.

The water moccasin, or cottonmouth, ranges from southern Virginia to Texas. Since it prefers to live in the swampy areas of that territory it very seldom makes contact with man. Its complete length at maturity can reach 6 feet and be as thick around as a big man's wrist. The name cottonmouth is derived from the cotton white interior of it's mouth which is exposed to view when it is aroused. If you are able to see the inside of this snake's mouth it would be a gross understatement to say that you are too close for comfort.

The most deadly venom is contained by the small, thin, brightly hued, blunt headed coral snake which ranges all the southeastern and southwestern states. Unfortunately there are a number of harmless snakes that resemble the coral snake. They are the scarlet and scarlet king snake, the western milk snake and the Arizona king snake. These snakes are mistakenly killed by people who believe them to be the deadly coral snake. The easiest way to distinguish the deadly coral snake from it's harmless impersonators is that the harmless snakes have a white or blotched belly while the deadly coral, or harlequin snakes have the colorful rings circling the entire body.

The coral snake will only bite when stepped on or touched and since it is primarily a nocturnal reptile it is seldom encountered by man.

The other poisonous reptile is the Gila monster which is found in the more arid regions of the United States, particularly in Arizona. This lizard feeds mostly on eggs and will only employ it's poison when defending itself. It is quite effective in killing poisonous snakes as it is immune to the

The water-dwelling-cottonmouth moccasin possesses an extremely toxic venom.

Coral snakes are very poisonous serpents, feeding on lizards and other snakes.

Copperheads are fearfully venomous pit-vipers, subsisting on warm-blooded prey.

venom of this enemy. The Gila monster reaches a growth of two feet and it is slow and sluggish enough to be captured by young boys who have not been fore-warned that it's bite can be fatal.

Unbelievable as it may seem, the bite of the non-poisonous snake causes as much damage if not more, than the bite of the poisonous variety. The reason is simply that the persons bitten will usually panic and injure themselves or develop a heart seizure that kills them.

Even the bite of a poisonous snake does not have to prove fatal if quick action is taken. The first thing that the person bitten must remember is to **REMAIN CALM, DON'T GET EXCITED, DON'T START RUNNING, LIE DOWN!** Then follow the instructions listed herein.

An invaluable aid in snake country.

1. Take a belt, rope or some piece of material which can be used as a tourniquet. Apply the tourniquet about two or three inches above the bite. If the wound is below the knee or on the arm below the elbow a second tourniquet should be applied above the knee or the elbow. This will further retard blood circulation.

2. Coat the wound area with anti-septic. If no antiseptic is available, soap and water will suffice.

3. Make an incision, not more than 1/8 of an inch deep, over each fang hole. **DO NOT MAKE AN X SHAPE INCISION!** The incision should be parallel to the · wound. The razor or knife should be sterilized. This can be done in the campfire or by using a match or cigarette lighter.

4. If suction cups are not available do not hesitate to suck the wounded area by mouth. **SPIT THE POISON OUT!.** Small amounts of the poison will do no harm if they should be ingested. **IF YOU HAVE AN OPEN SORE IN YOUR MOUTH OR A DIGESTIVE PROBLEM (ULCERS) DO NOT SUCK A SNAKE BITE WOUND!**

5. Loosen the tourniquet every few minutes and continue to suck out the poison.

6. Once every hour, for the first two or three hours, the area

The all-terrain mountaineer boot: comfortable, reliable, rugged.

under treatment should be kept moist and cool by using saline packs. This is done between the suction treatment.

7. To retard the flow of blood, ice packs should be placed on the wound. This will slow the spread of the venom and hold down the swelling.

8. Keep reassuring the victim of the snake bite and reminding him that he should take it easy. Remain calm and don't get excited.

A snake bite kit should be standard equipment for all campers. Snake bite kits have proven to be effective in many cases. Don't wait until it is too late to get one. The kit that has proven to be very effective is marketed by Cutter Laboratories, Inc., Berkeley, California 94710.

INSECTS

It is impossible to go on a camping trip and be totally free of insects. But with all the spray, liquid and stick insecticides that are marketed today there is no excuse for a camping trip to be a total disaster just because of insects. Gnats, mosquitoes, little black flies, houseflies, sand flies and midges cannot be completely eliminated with these insecticides but they can be brought down to a tolerable level. The blood flies, deer or horsefly, can inflict a very nasty bite, they they are sluggish little beasts and they are not hard to swat. The bites from these insects should be treated with a mild disinfectant or alcohol.

Bees will sting when they are provoked. Do not swat at them or attempt to investigate their hives or nests. The wasp and hornet can

51

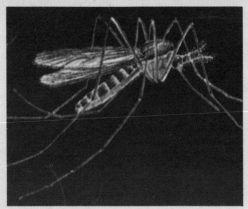

One species of Aedes Mosquito is
capable of transmitting Yellow Fever.

not only be painful but for those
people who have an allergy to
their venom it can prove fatal.
The yellow jacket is a ground
nesting bee. When searching out a
campsite it is suggested that you
do not set up your camp in an
area where you can see them
buzzing around. The sting of the
honeybee can be very irritating as
he leaves his stinger behind in
your skin. This barb must be removed in order to stop the pain
and irritation. All bee stings
should be treated at once with
alcohol or a paste made of baking
soda. If neither of these two items
is available mud should be applied to the area. The person who
has been stung should sit down
and not move about for 30 to 60
minutes.

The insects that can really
wreck a camping trip are the ants.
I don't have any evidence of an
ant bite being poisonous but they
can be painful. One way of not
encouraging ants is to be very
careful with food. This is not very

difficult since most foods are kept
in plastic containers or covered
with plastic wrap. Wherever you
go you will find ants and if you
keep the area as free of food as
possible you will not be bothered
by them unless you happen to
pitch your tent over one of their
nests. The bite of the fire ant is
probably the most painful of ant
bites. It feels as though someone
had touched you with a hot
poker. The fire ant is reddish
brown and ranges the open woods
and fields from the Carolinas to
the Gulf Coast. Ant bites should
be treated with cold applications
and alcohol.

Ticks are sneaky little buggers.
They latch on to you and dig their
heads into your body without
your ever knowing it. They are
bloodsuckers and if not removed
properly can cause infections.
They live in tall grass and low
bushes and are more prone to
attack your dog but that does not
mean they don't like the blood of
human beings. You must check

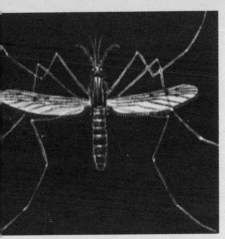

Three-pronged beak, buzzing, tilted stance, beware! Female Anopheles, malaria!

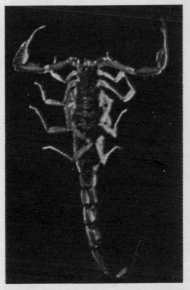

A scorpion's sting is toxic, check all shoes and bedding for this customer.

House fly: most common, dirty, disease carrying insect pest in the world.

yourself and your animal at least once every day. If one is found the odds are that there are more. Do not try to pick it off as the head separates from the body very easily and can remain inside the skin. The heat of a cigarette or match will make the tick back out as will a drop of gasoline, kerosene or rubbing alcohol. All tick bites should be treated with a disinfectant.

Dry grass, leaves and hay, hide mites or chiggers. They live mostly in the deep south. These insects are so tiny that the individual being bitten very often only thinks he has a rash. The itch they cause can be nerve wracking and if scratched can cause serious infections. Mites, or chiggers, can be washed off with brown or green soap and the itch can be relieved by using calamine lotion, alcohol, ammonia or a paste made with baking soda.

A common belief is that the only poisonous spider is the female black widow. That is not true. All spider bites are poisonous but very few are harmful to human beings. The most toxic and therefore the one that will cause a reaction in human beings, is the female black widow. The reaction from the bite of a female black widow will set in in 1 hour and the symptoms are severe abdominal cramps. If you know that you or a member of your party has been bitten by a black widow, medical attention should be sought at once. **DO NOT WAIT FOR THE CRAMPS TO START BEFORE SEEKING MEDICAL ADVICE!** The female black widow is distinguishable from other spiders by the crimson hourglass marking on her underside. Home for this 8 legged arthropod is in weedy fields or dry sheltered places.

The ugliest and most fearful looking of the spiders is the Tarantula who makes its home in the southwestern deserts. Although they rarely bite it is best to seek medical attention if you should be the unlucky recipient of it's attentions.

Another poisonous insect which makes it's home in the desert, as well as in sunny Florida, is the scorpion. They live under rocks and dark corners. If you do any desert camping it is recommended that you check your bedding every night before entering it and also to shake out your shoes every morning before putting them on. A scorpion sting is very toxic and will usually leave an infected wound that is very slow to heal.

Some other methods of repelling annoying insects, besides those already suggested, are placing wet grass on top of a fire to create smoke or placing burning punk at various intervals around the camp. These two methods might repel you as well as the insects.

WILDLIFE

There may not be any lions or tigers in the United States outside of the zoos, but that does not mean that the wildlife that we do have cannot be very dangerous. Many a camper has inflicted painful wounds on one or more of his children when he found and captured a rabbit and decided to let one of the youngsters hold the animal. Junior was just standing there holding the rabbit in his arms and lifting up it's ears so Daddy could take their picture when suddenly the rabbit wiggled around in such a way that he kicked Junior in the face or bit him on the finger. Yes, even the funny little bunny can be aggressive and cause injury.

Wild animals are not to be disturbed by you when you are a visitor in their domain. You are a stranger who is visiting without an invitation, you are just dropping in for a short visit. Do not impose on their hospitality by trying to capture them or tamper with their young. They will allow you the freedom of their home and the peace and tranquility that prevails if you do not become an overbearing guest. If you are alert you will be able to photograph them without any objection on their part if you don't come too close to them. With the modern telescopic lens you should be able to get excellent pictures of the wildlife without having to be on top of them.

The deer is an elusive creature who can be photographed at dawn and dusk near streams or lakes when they go to quench their thirst. When driving at those hours of the day it is best to be alert as they might dash out in front of your car.

The skunk is an animal to be avoided at all times. It doesn't take much to aggravate him and his spray is a very potent weapon. He is a sharpshooter up to distances not exceeding ten feet. His spray can, if it gets into your eyes, not only damage the sensitive tissues but cause blindness as well. People with cardiac conditions have been known to have heart attacks from the aroma of his spray.

Porcupines do not shoot out their quills but they will stand them on end if you approach them and if you touch them you will regret it. This fellow is also very short tempered so give him a wide berth. If he gets the opportunity he will chew up your axe handle or any other wood object containing salt from dried perspiration you might leave lying around.

The woodchuck is a field dweller who farmers consider pests. This is because the woodchuck makes his home in a hole which he burrows in the farmers field. Many times farm animals such as cows, horses, etc. will step in these holes and break their legs so the farmers kill woodchucks at random. He is a very cute looking little animal and he and his family should give you some very nice pictures as they bob in and out of their burrow. Do not let your children stick their hands down into one of these woodchuck holes or permit your dog to dig into them. They will both come up with some very nasty bites.

The masked bandit of the outdoors is not the Lone Ranger but the very intelligent, curious and tricky raccoon. If your food is not properly protected when you are out of camp he will come right into a tent and find it and steal it. He can open up cannisters, remove the lids from garbage cans and if you should see him and be foolish enough to throw some food to him he will only return with more of his kind and rob you blind. Since they are very curious animals they can be tempted to come close to humans with food or shiny objects. Do not do any-

The raccoon is deceptively cute but capable of inflicting painful wounds.

thing so foolish, as they can inflict some very nasty wounds.

BEARS ARE VERY DANGEROUS ANIMALS. There is no such thing as a tame bear. Not even in a circus or on a television show. Brown Bears, Black Bears and Grizzly Bears have never been tamed. Trained yes! Never tamed! It is just amazing how many people are killed and mauled each year because they saw such a cute little bear in the National Park and they wanted to have their picture taken standing next to it. The number of children who are permanently disabled because of the stupidity of their parents trying to sit them on a bears back could make you sick just thinking about it. Carelessly wrapped food or the careless disposal of garbage will bring these dangerous beasts to your campsite. All food must be hung in closed plastic bags at least 8 feet off of the ground. All refuse must be burned or buried. If a bear does enter your campsite do not try to shoo him away by waving aprons or cloths at him or making crazy sounds. Get into your car and get away from there. Find a ranger and inform him of what is taking place at your campsite. If you try to handle this situation by yourself or with other members of your party you might all be killed. Then the rangers will have to find the bear and kill him.

The Coyote, or prairie wolf, is a plains animal whom you will always hear but rarely get a chance to see. He loves to sing to the moon and if you are camping anywhere near his home territory you will probably lose many a

The black bear is not the benign-looking, furry clown that he appears to be. Exercise caution because he's able to totally destroy you and your property.

good nights sleep listening to his serenade. The coyote is no danger to you but a relative of his, the Coy Dog is an ever increasing danger. Since the forests of America have been stripped the coyote has been able to range far from his native habitat. This has enabled him to come into contact with man's best friend, the dog. The coyote has mated with the dog producing an offspring that has no natural fear of man plus all the instincts of a wild animal. These Coy Dogs travel in packs and have been known to attack children as well as adults. You must be very wary of them.

The animal that can change the course of a river but will not bother you, if you don't bother him, is the beaver. He is a very versatile little creature who cuts his own lumber, builds his own damn and creates housing projects. If you come across a beaver's dam do not stick your hand down into it and try to catch the beaver. Those teeth that chop down trees can remove several fingers from your hand and in the case of a child the hand itself.

It will be a very rare instance if you see a wildcat, bobcat or cougar. They have a hyper-sensitive fear of man and they stay far away from him. If by some strange accident you should meet one another, the cat will disappear like a screaming bolt of lightning.

The only animal that I know of that kills for the sake of killing alone is the wolverine. This animal is found only in the coldest country such as you find in northern Canada or Alaska. It reaches a top weight of about 40 pounds and

has been known to attack and kill a bear. It will eat a porcupine. He will rip his way into a tent and find some way to enter any but the most tightly secured cabin. He will tear up and destroy an entire camp and then foul up the area as a calling card. The only reason that we mention the wolverine is that modern transportation is taking campers even into some very remote areas and it is very possible that some campers are going up into the very forbidding country where the wolverine makes his home. If you do go camping in those outlying territories it is suggested that you take a gun along with you even though you are not intending to do any hunting.

As we stated earlier most animals have a natural fear of man and they will try to avoid him at every opportunity. You must be suspicious of any animal that is willing to come up close to you. Deer, rabbits, squirrels, woodchucks, any animal that you can think of poses a terrible threat to you and your fellow campers if he seems to act tame and is willing to approach you. This animal may have RABIES. An animal infected by this disease loses his fear of man and if man is close by he may even try to cuddle up to him. Just because he is not foaming at the mouth does not mean he does not have the disease. He may not have reached that stage as yet. This does not mean that he cannot infect you with his bite or even by licking your hand. Rabies is a virus and you can become infected by the virus entering your body through a small cut on your hand or by sticking your finger in

Once again we admonish you to be careful! Coyotes are potentially dangerous—not merely causing fang damage but by possible transmission of rabies.

your mouth or you can even inhale it. If you or a member of your party has been bitten or approached too closely by a suspiciously acting wild animal it is best that you kill it, sever it's head and bring the head to the nearest health station or veterinarian. It is better in this instance to be an alarmist and play it safe than to try to gloss over the incident. These precautions should be taken even in areas where the health authorities claim they haven't had a case of rabies in years. Yours could be the case that could break that record and you don't want to find out about it when it is too late.

CAMP HYGIENE

There is no big secret to cleanliness in camp. Organization is the key word at camp as well as at home. Individual responsibility can cut the overall cleaning time to just a little more than a half hour daily. The following check list of Do's and Don'ts should help ease your daily chores.

DO: . . .Wash all cooking and eating utensils immediately after each meal. Burn all paper dishes.

DO: . . .Sweep out the tent interior at least once every day.

DO: . . .Dig a bucket sized hole in the ground and fill it part way with stones or pebbles. This is where greasy dishwater is to be poured. Borax or soda ash will prevent any odor from forming.

DO: . . .Air out all blankets, sleeping bags and sleeping bag liners during sunny days only. This should be done particularly after a spell of bad or damp weather.

DO: . . .Place all axes, hatchets, shovels, flashlights, first aid kits and all other items that might be used by more than one member of the party in one specific place and be sure that they are returned to that place immediately after use.

DO: . . .Prevent dirtying up the interior of the tent with muddy shoes or boots by placing a mat made of tree branches in front of the tent entrance for scraping the bottom of the boots.

DO: . . .Replace all left over food items that are still edible in aluminum foil or plastic containers as soon as you are finished eating.

DO: . . .Place all leftover food items that are no longer useable in the trash cans that are provided in state or federal parks. Be sure that this garbage is in paper or plastic bags. If in the wilderness dig a trench and bury all garbage.

DO NOT . . .Pour liquid wastes into streams and lakes.

DO NOT . . .Bury bottles or tin cans with your garbage. If trash cans are not available take all soda bottles and cans back home and dispose of them in your usual manner at home.

DO NOT . . .Chop down any live trees.

DO: . . .Carry a chemical toilet along on any extended trips to isolated areas. It will save you digging a latrine and calm any fears you might have about polluting the area.

DO: . . .Cover up that hole which was dug for the greasy dish water. The practice of good housekeeping at a campsite goes hand in hand with good conservation practices. Conservation is something to which a great deal of lip service is paid. A great many people do a lot of talking about pure water, pure air, and clean campgrounds. I have been to campsites where the previous camper was pulling out as I was pulling in. The campsite looked as though it was the town dump. Soda and beer cans strewn all over the place, paper wrappers, cup and plates blowing hither and yonder in the wind and I recalled seeing two bumper stickers on the back of the trailer that had just pulled out of the campsite. They stated, "DON'T LITTER" and "CONSERVATION MEANS YOU." I presume that the previous camper and his family thought they were placing "NO SMOKING" bumper stickers on the back of their vehicle. I only know that I cussed that man and his party for the two and a half hours it took my camping party to clean up his mess.

ACCIDENT PREVENTION

No matter how often or how many years you have gone on camping trips you must realize that you are primarily an urban or suburban dweller and the outdoors can no longer be considered a part of your natural environment. You are conditioned to traffic lights, mowing lawns, central heating, paved roads, automated elevators, refrigerators, super markets, paved sidewalks, nearby docters and hospitals and sundry other modern conveniences which are lacking in wilderness camping. Even the nearby state park which has many modern conveniences, or is not too far from them, can be a hostile environment for modern man. It is hostile because you are removed from your natural surroundings. You are as out of place in the wilderness as a deer would be on the streets of your home town. The difference between you and the deer is that the deer would be frightened to death if he were suddenly placed on even the quietest street in your community while you, freed from the dangers of dodging traffic, let down your guard and romp through the forests without the slightest regard for the simplest safety precautions. The sad part is that injuries in the wilderness are usually a result of carelessness. Sprained ankles, torn ligaments and broken bones, blisters and cuts and bruises are a plague to the camper who doesn't approach his stay in the wilderness with just a touch of common sense.

A. Tent stakes and tent ropes can be booby traps during the day as well as at night. Tripping over either one can cause a painful injury. Strips of colored rag or ribbon, white or red, tied on tent ropes will increase daytime visibility. Paint the stakes and dot the ropes with a radiant paint, such as Day-Glo, to keep them visible at night.

B. Blisters occur on the hands and the feet. Wielding an axe or digging a trench can work up some dandy blisters on hands that have been pushing nothing more than a pencil for 50 weeks of the year. Grabbing a hot pot or some other cooking utensil can cause severe finger and palm burns when the camper forgets that an open fire radiates more heat over a wider area than the gas or electric range at home. Your feet can blister when you wear shoes, boots or socks that are either too tight or too loose. New shoes and boots will do the same unless they are well broken in. The treatment for blisters in all cases is as follows. Sterilize the skin on the blister as well as the skin surrounding the blister. Soap and warm water is always best when no other sterilizing agent is available. Then sterilize a needle. (Don't burn yourself attempting to sterilize the needle.) This can be done in the fire or with a match or cigarette lighter. Puncture the blister with the needle around the edge and allow the blister to drain. Let it dry and then cover it with a bandaid or use gauze and adhesive tape. All blisters should be treated at once. The best treatment of all is the preventive medicine. Wear gloves when digging or chopping wood. Wear gloves when removing cooking utensils from the fire and wear perfectly form fitting shoes, boots or socks.

C. Prevent cuts, gashes and possible amputations by using axes, hatchets, knives and any other cutting instrument in the prescribed safe manner. Do not use any of these implements for any other purpose except that which they were made for. In straight English, DON'T try to open a can of beans with a butcher knife or use an axe as a bottle opener. When these implements are not being used they should be in their carrying cases or sheaths.

D. Catching a cold can not only ruin a camping trip but you can carry it around long after the vacation is over. The night time, when you are sleeping and the dampness and evening chill sets in, is the time when you are liable to catch a cold. Whether you are sleeping on a cot or an air mattress it is best to line them both with one or two blankets or a couple of layers of newspapers. It doesn't matter how many blankets you have on top of you, you might just as well be uncovered as to neglect covering the area that you are sleeping on. Your feet can be kept warm by filling your canteen with hot water and covering it with a towel and then placing it under your blanket. Hot rocks or bricks from the fire can also keep your feet warm. Just don't forget to cover them with a towel. I have found that a lightweight scarf wrapped around my neck and tucked inside my shirt protects my neck and chest from the cold. For minor sore throats you can use salt and water or baking soda mixed with water. They can also be used for brushing your teeth in case you forget the toothpaste, or for washing out minor cuts and scratches.

E. Many of the items taken on camping trips can be deadly weapons after they are used if they are not disposed of properly. Not only could they injure one of your party but someone who might use the camping area after you are gone. I am referring to glass jars and tin cans. They could be olive jars, soda bottles, cans of soda or soup cans. Many camping manuals recommend that all campers should dig a deep hole and place all of this dangerous refuse in it and cover it up when they leave. Glass and tin are supposed to be reclaimed by the earth since they are all made from natural elements. I don't recommend this as it will take thousands of years before any final reaction takes place on the glass or the tin. I believe that they should be disposed of in the containers that are provided in most state and national parks. If you are in a complete wilderness area and these containers are not avaiable to you then make sure that they are collected after each meal and placed in a safe place and removed from the park where you can dispose of them either at home or presented to some organization that sells them for reclamation and re-use.

F. One or even two flashlights are not enough on a camping trip. Every member of the expedition should have a personal flashlight and it should be kept at the side of his sleeping space during the night. Moving around in the darkness without a flashlight when nature calls can be very dangerous. Don't forget extra bulbs and batteries.

G. Do not set up camp until you have checked the overhanging branches of the trees. Dead branches can cause serious injury if they should fall during the night. If you spot one, it can be pulled down with a rope and used for firewood.

H. Quicksand, bogs and mire are only dangerous when you are ignorant of how to deal with them in case you should be caught in them. The first rule of course is not to get caught in them. You can avoid this danger by being familiarized with the area in which you are going to camp, through maps and other materials furnished by the state and national parks. If you should be trapped in any of the above three elements the following rules will get you out safe and sound. Be sure that you drill yourself and every member of your family or party on how to deal with this situation.

1...DON'T PANIC!

2...DON'T STRUGGLE!

3...DON'T TRY TO PULL YOUR FEET UP! Trying to pull your feet up will only pull you down faster.

4...DO LEAN FORWARD ON YOUR CHEST AND STOMACH AS SOON AS YOU REALIZE THAT YOU ARE TRAPPED!

5...LIE AS FLAT AS POSSIBLE IN THE QUICKSAND OR MIRE!

6...YOUR LEGS WILL BEGIN TO COME TO THE SURFACE AS SOON AS THE WEIGHT OF THE BODY HAS BEEN REMOVED FROM THEM!

7...STRETCH YOUR LEGS BEHIND YOU UNTIL THE ENTIRE BODY IS IN A HORIZONTAL POSITION ON THE MIRE OR QUICKSAND!

8...THE AIR IN YOUR LUNGS WILL KEEP YOU FLOATING AS SOON AS THE DOWNWARD SUCTION ON YOUR LEGS HAS BEEN ELIMINATED!

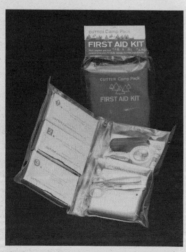

In assembling your camp gear, it's not unwise to pack a first aid kit, first.

9...USING YOUR ARMS IN A SLOW STEADY BREAST STROKE, JUST LIKE SWIMMING, WILL BRING YOU TO SAFE GROUND. DO NOT KICK THE LEGS!

I. A FIRST AID KIT is as necessary as your clothing and food. Never go camping without one.

J. If you are going to be camping in an area where you have the slightest doubt about the water make sure that you take along an approved water purification kit.

K. The serious consequences of sunburn and windburn are often ignored by the camper. Don't take any chances. NOT EVEN ON A CLOUDY DAY! Blonds, redheads and children in particular should be constantly reminded to use suntan lotion on the exposed portions of their bodies. Longsleeved shirts, slacks and wide brimmed hats of lightweight materials will do more to prevent sunburn and windburn than all the suntan lotions combined. Dark glasses are a must to protect the eyes from the sun and the glare. Colored lenses should be avoided. Particularly yellow lenses. A neutral density lens is the best. Your dog is not immune to sunburn or windburn, especially the little pooch whose owner likes to change the animals natural hairdo. If your dog has been clipped or trimmed we suggest that you board him when you go on your trip. A sun or windburn would only torture the poor animal.

L. FOOD POISONING CAN BE FATAL! It is also unnecessary. You can tell if canned goods are spoiled simply by checking the ends of the can. If they are bulged, THROW IT AWAY! If your other food seem to have developed an odor that you do not like, don't take any chances. THROW IT AWAY! If your meats have any discoloration, THROW THEM AWAY! If you are the least bit suspicious of anything that you are about to prepare to eat, GET RID OF IT! BOTULISM KILLS!

M. Cuts, wounds and abrasions should be thoroughly cleansed. If you have the proper first aid kit a goodly supply of antiseptic will be on hand. If you do not have a first aid kit it is a good thing to remember that soap and water work as well as most antiseptics. The flow of blood from a bleeding wound can be staunched by applying the membrane of a fresh egg to the wound once it has been cleansed. First you hold the wound closed and then you apply the egg membrane over the cut. The egg membrane will dry and pull the edges of the wound together thus stopping the flow of blood. The egg membrane will keep the wound sterile and aid in healing.

N. The tourniquet which must be used to staunch a flow of blood or in the case of snake bite must be loosened every 15 minutes to restore circulation to the area cut off from the blood supply. If this is not done, permanent injury can be inflicted on the affected tissues and a gangrene infection could take place which might mean the limb would have to be amputated.   REMEMBER!!! LOOSEN THE TOURNIQUET EVERY 15 MINUTES!!!

PERSONAL EQUIPMENT

Personal equipment is naturally the responsibility of each individual going on a camping trip. The equipment that each person needs for himself has to do with his or her own tastes as well as personal requirements. Make out a personal check list and let common sense be your guide. Remember that you are going on a camping expedition and not a fashion show. This last remark is pointed straight at the ladies who will sometimes bring along fingernail polish, cleansing cream, emery boards and all kinds of do-dads that only take up precious space. Cleansing creams, which the ladies use on their faces will only cause more trouble than it is worth. It will attract bugs, mosquitoes, gnats, etc., which will not only fill up the cold cream jar but will bite the dickens out of the lady's face during the night so that the next morning she will look like a magazine add of a girl with acne before she used the advertised product. Soap and water is the best cleanser and soap doesn't take up as much room as a cold cream jar. All kinds of cosmetics are a pain on a camping trip. Not only to the one who uses them, but to the other campers who will have to lend things to the lady who brought them in place of the absolute necessities.

Those tight form-fitting stretch-pants may look great on the lady who is overseeing a backyard cook-out but on a camping trip she is just asking for unnecessary scratches. Nobody is going to sit around the camp all day. The urge to get around and explore must take precedence over sheer boredom and when the lady in the stretch pants starts walking through the woods or the fields in those stretch pants the wild rose, berry and bramble bushes are going to do a job on her legs and thighs. She will look as though she has been worked over with a cat-o-nine tails before she has moved ten minutes outside of the camp.

The man in the family doesn't escape unscathed here. He is sure that he is using common sense when he packs his personal belongings for the trip. And he is sure `that his common sense is going to insure his comfort. What does he pack? He packs his very comfortable house slippers. What is wrong with that? The soles of house slippers are too soft. Stepping outside the tent at night and stepping on a pebble or a twig can inflict a very painful and almost crippling bruise on the underside of the foot. A pair of hard soled moccasins or boat sneakers would be more practical.

There are ready-pack personal necessities available for sale in all sporting goods stores. You may not want to buy them or you may not be completely satisfied with what the pre-packaged kit includes but you can check them over and supply yourself with what you think would make up a great personal equipment package. In the meantime you can look over the list that is prepared here and delete those items that you don't think apply to you or add to the list at your discretion.

TOOTHBRUSH, TOOTHPASTE, SOAP, WASH CLOTH, TOWEL. (Extra wash cloths and towels should be included.)

SHAVING KIT, SHAVING CREAM, MIRROR. (Metal reflector preferable.)

EXTRA SOCKS.

EXTRA SHOES. (Comfortable, as suggested.)

WRISTWATCHES.

FLASHLIGHTS. (One for each person. Extra bulbs and batteries.)

CAMERA AND FILM.

EXTRA SWEATERS.

EXTRA JACKETS.

EXTRA RAINCOAT AND/OR PONCHO.

HATS, wide brimmed. CAPS, peaked.

HANDKERCHIEFS AND/OR FACIAL TISSUES.

NOTEBOOKS AND PENCILS.

INSECT REPELLENTS

MATCHES AND CIGARETTE LIGHTERS, PLUS LIGHTER FLUID.

PERSONAL DEODORANTS (Unscented).

These are merely suggestions. Where a special diet is concerned the check list must be made out by the party who must abide by that diet.

Camping is supposed to be fun and fun means comfort, therefore comfort must be the prime consideration when making out your check list. Don't under pack and don't over pack and you'll find some pleasant experiences in our wilderness areas.

AT EASE IN CAMP

Once again the thought of comfort rears it's beautiful head and we in turn offer what we have found to add to our comfort while basking in the arms of nature. No matter how many modern conveniences we take into the wilderness with us we are still trying to return to the simple existence which we believe our pioneering forefathers found so pleasurable. But our pioneer forefathers were bringing civilization to the new world. They built houses and cultivated the land. The life that we are actually looking for is that which was led by the mountain men. The men who braved the wilderness to trap animals for their fur. Their was an extended camping trip that would sometimes last up to two or three years. These mountain men were the rugged individuals whose roof was the stars and whose bed was the earth. They survived the elements to bring back the pelts of the beaver and the otter to the cities of the new world. But they never stayed long at the little outposts that they considered to be civilization. They would leave within days of their return to go back to the forests and mountains

where the tread of a human foot had never before been felt or heard and if it was it was just the footstep of an individual American Indian.

It was the American Indian who taught this trapper, this mountain man how to survive against nature's savage beauty in this new land and it is the American Indian whom we can thank for passing this information on to the strangers who came before us.

One of the pieces of information that the American Indian gave us has been utilized all over the world and very few people remember them for their gift. They invented the hammock. How many sailors do you think have realized over the centuries that they were sleeping on an item invented, who knows when, by an American Aborigine. The hammock may not be an indispensible camping item but it certainly does add to the campers comfort. Folded up, it is compact enough to be carried in a backpack so it isn't even inconvenient to carry on your trip.

One of the most neglected of creature comforts, where camping is concerned is the air mattress. For some reason most people only think of them as toys to be used in swimming pools or in the Gulf of Mexico but never as something to sleep on while on a camping trip. They are compact and easy to carry when deflated and when ready for use they can be inflated quickly with an aerosol inflator or a small bicycle tire pump without very much effort. The comfort of sleeping on an air mattress on a camping trip is second only to sleeping on a water bed back home. When used in the water, inflate to capacity. When used for sleeping, inflate to half capacity.

Many a camper goes without a Poncho because of the cost factor. Perhaps this suggestion will eliminate the Poncho shortage although we don't think that the Poncho manufacturers will thank us for giving it to you. A Poncho can be made at home by even the most inept sewing needle handler. Use an old blanket, but one that will still see a lot of service, and cut a slit diagonally into the center. Cross stitch the slit and then sew on a couple of press-fasteners on either side of it. Now you have a double threat piece of equipment. You have a Poncho to ward off the chill at night when you are sitting around the campfire and a blanket to keep you warm when you are sleeping. When used as a blanket you use the press-fasteners to close the slit in the blanket.

CATEGORIZED CHECK LIST

Rather than just making a check list with the items listed in a haphazard manner it is best to categorize your list and then place the items on that list which fit under that category. In this way it will also be easy to give each individual member a list for which he will be personally responsible. You may add or delete from the following list according to your own personal tastes and needs. These categories are not necessarily listed in order of importance.

AUTOMOBILE:
Full gas tank.

Extra 5 gallon metal jerry can filled with gas.
Two extra quart cans of oil.
Pouring spout for oil cans.
Battery fully charged.
Battery terminals clean and free of corrosive materials.
Battery jumper cables.
Extra spark plugs.
Engine tuned up.
All four tires with good rubber on them and properly inflated.
Good spare tire. Check to see if it is inflated.
Heater and defroster in proper working condition.
Good wiper blades.
Extra set of windshield wiper blades.
Windshield washer sprayer filled and in working condition.
Extra gallon of windshield washer liquid.
Extra car fuses.
Emergency road flares.
Drivers licenses for all drivers.
Automobile registration.
Insurance certificate.
Trailer registration.
Personal identification.
Small amount of cash.
Travelers checks.
Credit cards.

SHELTER:
Tent.
Tent poles.
Tent stakes.
Tent ropes.
Floor mat for tent.
Door mat for tent.
Extra tarpaulin.
Sleeping bags.
Cots.
Air mattresses.

Hammocks.
Blankets.
Mosquito nets.
Ponchos.

LIGHTING:

Flashlights.
Extra flashlight batteries.
Extra flashlight bulbs.
Lanterns.
Fuel for lanterns.
Small funnel.
Box of Candles.
Matches (in waterproof containers).
Cigarette lighter. (windproof)
Extra lighter fluid, flints and wicks.

RECREATION:

Fishing rods and reels.
Tackle box. (fully equipped: lures, etc.)
Fishing nets.
Bathing suits.
Butterfly nets.
Magnifying glass.
Binoculars.
Bird watchers manual.
Insect identification manual.
Tree and shrub identification manual.
Camera.
Film.
Flash cubes. (For camera.)
Extra batteries. (For flash cubes.)

COOKING AND EATING:

Stove.
Oven.
Fuel for stove. (Gasoline, propane, what-have-you.)
Barbecue grill and all accessories.
Charcoal.

Charcoal fire starter.
Pots, pans, dishes.
Aluminum foil.
Wax paper.
Table cloth.
Paper towels or napkins.
Can opener.
Folding table and chairs.
Eating utensils. (Knives, forks, spoons.)
Large spoons. (For serving and stirring.)
Extra plastic containers for leftovers.
Pot holders or asbestos gloves.

Propane lantern: steady, reliable light. Windproof, long-burning, clean.

The two-burner, propane gas, campstove is a compact, versatile cooking unit.

GENERAL CLEANING:

Dish pan or water pail.
Scouring pads, dish washing soap.
Dish cloths.
Dish towels.
Straw broom.
Dust Pan.
Whisk broom.
Clothesline and clothespins.
Laundry detergent. (Biodegradable.)

GENERAL CAMPING NEEDS:

Axe.
Hatchet.
Shovel.
Hunting Knife.
Saw.
Extra rope.
Sewing kit.
Scissors.
Hammer.
Nails.
Thumbtacks.
Safety pins.
First aid kit.
Water purifying kit.

In most camping manuals they recommend that you bring along portable radios and television sets. They even include games such as volley ball and badminton. The man who goes on a camping trip with his family and takes along the above mentioned items is not interested in the outdoors nor is he interested in getting to know his children. The wilderness is no place for television or blasting radios. That is the place where you can find some peace and quiet. The wilderness is where you can leave the cares and noise of the world behind you and there is no necessity to carry blaring rock and roll music or T.V. commercials into the wilderness to disturb the stillness and scare the wildlife half to death. The wilderness is a place where you can sit back and listen and teach your children to listen and to become observant of what is going on around them. Let them learn to distinguish the difference between a cricket and a bird. Take them on a hike to collect leaves, rocks or fossils. Teach them the many varieties of trees and bushes. Show them how interesting it can be to watch birds or study the ants and other crawling insects. The raucous sound of radio, television or children playing backyard games in the wilderness can be heard for miles in all directions. You not only disturb the wildlife but other campers who are camped anywhere near you. A small transistor radio is really all that you need to keep you informed of local weather conditions. It should never be turned on at any other time except when the weather forecasts are being broadcast. Your very presence in the wilderness is abhorant to the wildlife who make their home there. Don't add insult to injury by bringing radios, televisions and backyard games to polute the beauty of nature's silence. ●

CHAPTER 8

SURVIVAL

*A basic urge in man is survival. Yet, having the desire
to survive does not necessarily give one the ability to do so.*

■ No one ever plans a trip where his survival is going to be placed on the line. No one plans to get lost or stranded in the wilderness but every year we read about hundreds of people who are lost somewhere in our wilderness parks which necessitates huge search and rescue operations which in turn involves scores of people which in turn costs time and money. For the person who is the object of the search, the people, time and money are of little importance. He wants to sur-

vive and be rescued as quickly as possible. Our object here is to give you the information that will help you to survive until rescue arrives.

The first, and most important reaction that must be overcome is panic. If you cannot control panic then any information that we give you will be useless. If you cannot control panic you cannot survive. A person can survive in the wilderness indefinitely if he does not allow panic to take the upper hand. The first reaction to panic seems to be to run off in some haphazard direction. Running in panic can lead to a bad sprain or broken bone which can only add problems to our immediate objective. If you are fortunate enough not to injure yourself you still have the added obstacle that is brought on by panic and that is exhaustion. Exhaustion brought on by panic can so weaken an individual that he will not have the strength to stand on his own two feet no less to do the work that is necessary to survive. If possible, the first thing that you must do upon the realization that you are lost is to sit down and relax for about ten or fifteen minutes. There is no rush for you to do anything. It is not even necessary at this time for you to take stock of your situation. You will just sit there and be calm for that length of time. Even if you are not overcome by panic relaxing at this time is the best thing for you. After those ten or fifteen minutes have passed, you can get on about the business of survival.

The best rule, of course, is not to get lost. This sounds silly but most people get lost because they wandered too far away from their campsite. So, don't walk out of sight or hearing distance of your camp. The other rule is not to leave the campsite by yourself. The old Buddy System used by the Boy Scouts where every activity, swimming, hiking, exploring, is done in pairs is a very good rule to go by. Besides the old cliche of "Two heads being better than one", an experience shared with a companion is always more pleasurable.

First of all you should always be familiar with the area in which you are going to set up your camp before you ever get there. This can be done with maps supplied by the parks and by speaking to people who might have camped in that area before you. These maps should always be in a handy place in the camp. You should study them before leaving your campsite.

Inform the other members of your party when you are going to leave the campsite and tell them how long you expect to be away from the camp. They should also know the general area that you intend to explore. Then if you have not returned to the camp within one hour of the time that you set, they can begin to make plans for a preliminary search party which should leave camp two hours after your expected time of return.

One of the items that you should carry with you when you leave the campsite is a large spool of brightly colored ribbon. This should be cut and tied to the trees at eye level as you wend your way away from the camp. Once you are out of sight of the camp, every tree is going to look alike and the ribbon will help you to find your way back. Make sure that the color ribbon that you choose will not blend in with the foliage. Please remove the ribbon on your way back to the camp.

Every member of your camping party should have his own personal compass and he should be instructed in its proper use. The compass should be carried by every person at all times. If for some reason the compass is

Learning to use a compass correctly is a must for all wise campers.

dashing around in circles. After you have relaxed and calmed your first fears, stand up and look around you. Decide which direction you are going to travel in. Then sight a specific object in that direction and walk straight to it. Once you arrive at that object you should relax for a moment. Then pick out another object that is aligned in a straight line with the place that you have just left. Walk toward that. If the direction you have chosen was selected by compass or wristwatch and you can keep sighting those straight line objects you will reach your destination without any problems.

There are times when it makes more sense to stay exactly where you are rather than try to find your way out at once. One of those times is when you find that you are lost and it is getting dark. This should not in any way disturb you. You will just make use of the available light to make yourself comfortable through the night. When you are back in civilization you will tell everyone how you used your head and kept yourself warm and even slept like a babe in his mother's arms. The first thing that you must find is a clearing. The clearing should be on high ground. You will then gather leaves, kindling and firewood and start a fire. Next, you will prepare your shelter. This will protect you from wind and rain. Pine, hemlock and evergreen branches as well as laurel or rhododendron sprigs can be used to make a makeshift tent that will protect you even in a heavy rainstorm. You can even make them into a lean-to against a large rock

broken or lost then a wrist watch can make a good substitute. Unlike the compass, which points North, you must remember that the wrist watch points South. The wrist watch must be held level; then point the hour hand towards the sun. Now draw a line half way between 12 and the hour hand. This is done clockwise from the 12. This line will point due South. If you are taking your reading at 4:00 P.M. the line pointing due South would cross the number 2 on your wristwatch.

Whether you are panic stricken or calm as a cucumber it is normal for both man and wild animal to walk in circles. This has been proven by scientific research so don't think that you are going to be the exception to what science has proven without any doubts. It was proven that the Donner Party wandered in complete circles even to the point of going over their own trail time and time again. Sitting down and relaxing will help you avoid panic as well as or against a tree. The ground under an evergreen tree or a rhododendron can be totally dry even after a cloudburst so there is no need for you to get wet. If you were smart, you had your survival kit along with you when you left camp. It is compact enough for you to carry without any discomfort at all. In that survival kit there is a full length plastic raincoat that weighs less than two ounces. This can be opened up and with the branches that we have just suggested, made into a tent. Your bedding is simple. You can scrape up leaves and pine needles into a pile and it will be like sleeping on a foam rubber mattress at home.

Now you have shelter with your tent and warmth with your fire. Your next concern is food and drink. If you have your Survival kit with you, food will be no problem as the kit contains an emergency supply of concentrated foods as well as the basic essentials for you to get in some fishing while you are lost. The kit contains a line and hooks. The rod of course can be made from the small branch of a tree. Bait is simple enough to get. There are plenty of grubs under dead logs and if you are near a supply of water you can heat some up in your canteen, (let's hope that you were smart enough to take a canteen full of water along with you), and after it is warm you just pour it over the soil and any earth worms that are there will come to the surface. The fish will make an excellent meal. Particularly when they have been cleaned with the knife that should be in its sheath

that is attached to your belt or the one that is in your survival kit. If you did not bring your survival kit and you don't have any concentrated food or fishing line, food is still not a problem for you. Since we are talking about being lost in the mountains we know that you are going to be somewhere near water. Creeks and streams are the home of frogs, crawfish or turtles. These items are considered to be delicacies in many fancy restaurants and they charge some very fancy prices for them. They are now yours for the taking. Then there are always locusts and dragon flies or even the grubs you cannot use for bait. They may not be very appetizing but they are nutritious. DO NOT EAT ANY BERRIES when you are lost. They could kill you. Birds can be eaten but they must be cooked very well done. Do not drink any water that you have not boiled in your canteen.

There are other foods available to you if you will just keep your head and look around you. You can start by eating dandelion. You should be able to find plenty of wild carrots or asparagus which when boiled up with fern sprouts can make an excellent vegetable soup.

Do not attempt to eat any mushrooms. They could be poisonous and they could make you very ill if not kill you. The only berry that we recommend for you to eat is the strawberry. There are no poisonous berries that resemble the strawberry and therefore it is perfectly safe to eat the wild strawberries that grow in abundance under your feet in the wilderness. If you see any squirrels or chipmunks you can watch just which nuts they are collecting and you can collect some of your own and eat them in perfect safety. So there you are with all that food available to you that you never before knew existed and all your fears about being lost have crumbled away.

Being lost in the desert presents a much different problem. Water is the primary concern and food is secondary. NEVER LEAVE A DESERT CAMPSITE WITHOUT A GOOD SUPPLY OF WATER! Remember to use it very sparingly. You can go without food for several days. No water in the hot desert puts survival on an hourly basis. If you remain calm and use your head you can even make water in the desert. The Solar Still is the desert water maker and it is included in the Desert Survival Kit. If you do not have a Desert Survival Kit with

Solar still showing concavity formed by weight of rock in center of plastic.

you when you are lost you can make your own Solar Still. The accompanying illustrations will show you how simple it is.

Now that we have shown you how simple and easy it is to survive in the wilderness if you keep your head and don't panic, let us inform you as to how you can

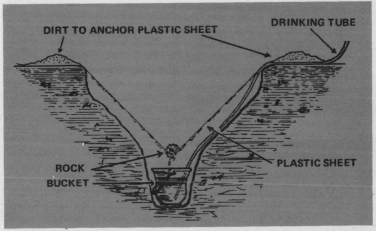

DIRT TO ANCHOR PLASTIC SHEET

DRINKING TUBE

ROCK

BUCKET

PLASTIC SHEET

Diagram of survival still: when heat from sun vaporizes water in the ground, the vapor rises, condensing on under side of plastic and trickles down into vessel.

assist the people who are looking to rescue you. They will be coming from two directions. They will be searching on the ground and in the air. Since you have no radio or signal flags how are you going to communicate with a helicopter pilot that you are the distressed individual he is searching for? Three fires burning in a clearing will inform the pilot that his search is over. If there is enough room for him to set down the helicopter you will be out of there in no time at all. If he cannot land he will inform the rescuers on the ground as to your location and he will probably stand by until they reach you.

Pay particular attention to the number THREE for the signal fires. THREE is the accepted international distress signal. THREE blasts on a whistle, THREE lusty shouts, THREE shots from a gun, THREE of anything that can be construed as a signal is the MAY-DAY or HELP ME of the wilderness. We suggest that a scout or police whistle be included in your SURVIVAL KIT because you could shout yourself hoarse and ruin your throat but blowing on a whistle will not hurt you or sap your energy. The United States Armed Forces also have specific distress signals. These signals can be stomped into the snow and they will appear black from the air or they can be layed out with wood, stones or strips of cloth. They should be no less than ten feet long. The number THREE though is understood by everybody to be a distress signal. This signal may not necessarily be used by you but it can be used by someone else and you will recognize the signal and rescue them.

You do not have to rush out and buy a SURVIVAL KIT. You can make up your own. Just remember that the items included should be compact and easy to carry.

GROUND-AIR EMERGENCY CODE

I 1. Require doctor — serious injuries	**II** 2. Require medical supplies	**X** 3. Unable to proceed	**F** 4. Require food and water	**≫** 5. Require firearms and ammunition	**K** 6. Indicate direction & proceed
↑ 7. Am proceeding in this direction	**I)** 8. Will attempt to take off	**⌐** 9. Aircraft badly damaged	**△** 10. Probably safe to land here	**LL** 11. All well	**L** 12. Require fuel and oil
N 13. No — negative	**Y** 14. Yes — affirmative	**⅃L** 15. Not understood	**W** 16. Require engineer	**□** 17. Require compass & map	**!** 18. Require signal lamp

Three-day life pack for emergency use. Food and water for one person for three days.

Tasty trail treat—four individual cans: jerky, candy, pemmican and protein drink.

FOOD SURVIVAL KIT:

1. Bouillon cubes or dehydrated soups.
2. Packets of instant coffee or tea.
3. Packets of powdered milk or cream.
4. Packets of salt and pepper.
5. Packets of sugar.
6. Concentrated chocolate or powdered chocolate.

The above named items are available in all supermarkets in pre-packaged foil or plastic and they will take up very little room in a shirt pocket. You could carry 5 or 6 of them and never notice the difference . . . until you need it. As long as the packages are not broken the food will last indefinitely.

ARTICLES FOR SURVIVAL KIT:

1. Waterproof wooden matches. (Dipping in paraffin waterproofs the matches.)
2. Cigarette lighter, filled. Extra wick and flint inside.
3. Suntan cream or lotion.
4. Small first aid kit.
5. Candle stub. Used for light or starting fire.
6. Fish hooks and length of fishing line.
7. Miniature sewing kit.
8. Safety pins.
9. Small first aid kit.
10. Plastic tape.
11. Single-edged razor blade.
12. Pocket knife.
13. Knife in sheath carried on belt at all times.
14. Compass.
15. Wristwatch.
16. Canteen filled with water carried on belt.
17. Flashlight. Carried on belt.
18. Lightweight plastic raincoat.
19. Area map.

This is very little weight to carry when you are going on a hike in the wilderness and it will

An absolute necessity for the touring camper is a well-delineated area map.

carry you through a very long and rough period should it become necessary. The most important point in survival is the one we admonished you about at the beginning of this section. **DO NOT PANIC!**

The car is a very wonderful invention indeed but it has probably been the cause of stranding more people than have ever been lost in the wilderness. A washed out road, a blizzard, a rock slide can suddenly become a survival situation. The car itself can have a mechanical failure that cannot be repaired on the spot or you may just have neglected to fill the tank and you have run out of gas at the wrong time and the wrong place.

This metal monster which you now feel like cussing is actually a huge survival kit and when you know what you are doing, it can assure your well-being.

As soon as you hear and feel that little sputter that tells you the car is running out of gas you should pull over to the side of the road. Don't wait until the car stops because the gas tank is thoroughly dry. You do not want a completely dry gas tank. The little gas that is left in the tank will help you to start a signal fire. DO NOT WALK AWAY FROM THE CAR unless you are positive that assistance is very close.

Now the question is, how can the car aid in your survival? You can use the any one of the following to provide shade if you are stranded in the desert. HOOD, DOOR PANELS, UPHOLSTERY AND FLOOR MATS. In cold weather stay inside the car or use the hub caps or sunvisors as sand

scoops to dig a hole so that you can bury yourself in the sand for warmth. If you do not have the where-with-all to make a fire you can take your spare tire and deflate it. Pour some gasoline on it and throw a match on it. It may smell something awful but it will burn for hours providing you with warmth as well as acting as a distress signal.

If you do not have emergency flares, matches or working cigarette lighter you can start a fire using the glass of the dome light cover or a headlight lens. (Not the sealed beam headlight). You can concentrate the sunlight using these lenses just as you did when you were a kid with a small magnifying glass.

You can make a powerful signal spotlight by removing one of the headlights and rewiring it to the battery. By dismounting the rear view or side view mirror you can signal for miles by reflecting the sunlight.

Protect yourself from sunburn by smearing the exposed parts of your body with oil and grease. It is messy but it will save you a lot of pain.

Grease can be blackened with burned rubber and spread under your eyes. This will protect your eyes from the glare of the sun and sand.

Burn some oil in one of the hubcaps. It will send up a smoke signal that will be seen many miles away.

So you see, that metal monster that let you down by not continuing to roll can really be of much more use in aiding your survival than you had ever believed. ●

78

CHAPTER 9

VALUABLE TIPS

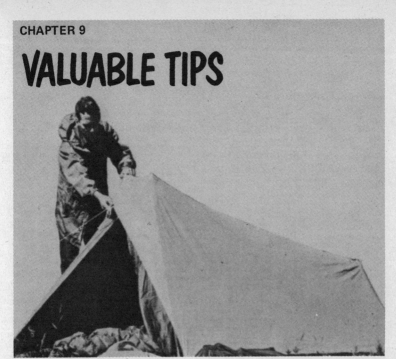

CAMPING TERMINOLOGY

There is a great deal of confusion among campers as to the various terms used to describe certain camping areas as well as recreational vehicles. A hue and cry is coming forth from the common folk for a standardization of camping terms so that two people can read the same government notice, trade magazine or direction sign and come up with the same understanding as to what it means. Listed below are some camping terms and their definitions which we hope will make a dent in the reigning confusion.

BACKPACKING: When all supplies for a camping trip are carried on the campers back. The term is usually applied when the individual goes on an extended camping trip into the wilderness using only his feet for transportation.

BACKPACKER: Term applied to the individual camper who goes backpacking.

BOTTLED GAS: This is Butane or Propane gas which is carried in cylinders and utilized for cooking on stoves and for lighting with lanterns especially adapted to use this gas.

CAMPER: Term used to describe an individual who goes camping. Also an abbreviated term to describe the recreation vehicle known as a truck camper or pickup camping truck.

CAMPGROUND: An undesignated number of campsites of a permanent nature in one camping establishment.

CAMP PARK: Term interchangeable with CAMPGROUND.

CAMPSITE: The area selected by a family or an individual to set up their tent in a wilderness area or a campground. This space could also be utilized by a trailer and still be classified as a campsite.

COOLER: An insulated box or bucket made of metal or plastic which will hold ice and therefore prevent food spoilage as well as chill drinks.

COUPLING: The connecting ball and socket arrangement that attaches a trailer to a car.

DOWN: An abbreviation of the word "Eiderdown". Eiderdown is duck and goose feathers. They make excellent insulation and are used in outdoor clothing and sleeping bags.

DUCK: Tent material of high quality.

DUMPING STATION: a designated area at many campgrounds to facilitate the emptying of recreational vehicle toilets.

DUTCH OVEN: A metal stove manufactured for use over an open camp fire. Excellent for stew, roasts and baking.

FIRE STARTERS: Commercially manufactured items impregnated with chemicals that assist in starting wood or charcoal fires.

GRILL: A metal rack on which cooking utensils will stand over an open campfire.

GUY LINE: Refers to any rope that maintains an upright structure. Used to sustain tent roof and walls.

HOLDING TANK: The built-in-tank in recreational vehicles that holds the waste materials from the kitchen sink and toilet.

HOOKUP: Well insulated electrical connectors as well as high pressure hoses for water and sewage facilities. These facilities are provided by most modern campgrounds.

IMPROVED CAMPSITE: A campground which provides modern facilities which can include picnic tables, fireplaces, grills, flush toilet, running water and a shopping center. This is the opposite of the Primitive campground which provides no facilities at all.

LATRINE: A hole in the ground used as a toilet facility.

LATRINE TENT: The hole in the ground toilet facility with a tent or tarpaulin enclosure.

MOTOR HOME: The living unit mounted on a truck which usually contains sleeping accommodations as well as stove, sink shower and possibly chemical toilet.

PACK ANIMAL: The three most commonly used pack animals in this country are the horse, donkey and mule. They carry supplies into the wilderness areas inaccessible to vehicles.

PACKSACK: Used by backpackers to carry supplies. Usually made of canvas.

PAD: Mattress made of lightweight foam rubber.

PICKUP CAMPER: A living unit mounted on a pickup truck.

PLAYGROUND: An area in a campground designated for sports. It sometimes contains swings and see-saws for the entertainment of small children.

PONCHO: A blanket, slit in the center so that the wearer can have the blanket on his shoulders and covering his body with his head through the slit.

POP TENT: An igloo shaped tent that opens like an umbrella and is held taut by metal spines.

PORTAGE: The transporting of canoes and gear overland by hand in order to avoid dangerous water or to go from one body of water to another.

PRIMITIVE: Campgrounds which provide no modern facilities. Usually a wilderness camp.

PRIVATE CAMPGROUNDS: This is private property owned by individuals or clubs and are not open to the public. Also private property owned by an individual who will rent campsites to the public.

REFLECTOR OVEN: A three sided open oven with a grill or shelf to hold cooking utensils mounted on two slanted sides. It is set up to face the fire and reflect the heat.

SELF-CONTAINED VEHICLE: A living unit mounted on, or pulled behind, a motor vehicle that contains sleeping units, kitchen and bathroom facilities as well as holding tanks, water supplies and power hookups.

SLIDE-IN CAMPER: A camper that can be set on or removed from a pickup truck.

TENT TRAILER: A metal trailer containing a collapsible tent. When opened the walls and roof of the tent are made of standard tent materials.

TRAILER COURT: An area that provides hook-up facilities for live-in trailer homes.

TRAIL TENT: A lightweight and compact tent that can be carried in a backpack.

TRAVEL TRAILER: Can range to sizes up to 30 feet. They are usually made of metal and contain all the luxury of home in a recreational vehicle.

TRUCK CAMPER: Same as pickup camper.

TUMPLINE: A length of soft but strong material that measures 3 inches wide by 18 inches long. The material is placed across the backpacker's forehead and attaches to the two upper corners of his backpack. It helps to ease the load on his shoulders and back.

UMBRELLA TENT: A large pop-tent.

WALK-TO-SITE: A campsite located in a wilderness area that can be reached only on foot.

WALL TENT: A high roofed tent with straight walls and plenty of floor space.

WILDERNESS: These are areas in our national forests and national parks where no wheeled vehicles of any kind are permitted. They can be reached only on foot, canoe or horseback. They contain no improved facilities.

ADVICE FOR THE NOVICE

The information put forth in this section can be used by both the individual and family who have never gone camping but have been thinking about it for a very long time but just haven't been able to screw up the courage to take the first step.

There are really two types of novices where camping is concerned. There is the one who has never gone on a family camping trip at all and there is the family where the man is the only one who has ever gone on a camping trip. All of the former and one of the latter seem to come up with the same arguments for not attempting the venture. The weather, insects and leaving the comforts of civilization seem to encompass everything that they have against camping.

A man who could not convince his wife to go on a camping trip before they had children certainly feels that he is batting his head up against a stone wall once the baby arrives. His wife can't see herself in what she considers to be primitive living conditions with an infant.

Whether you are a family man or not or whether you are a family with or without children there is a way to break the ice without jumping into the cold water.

Many state parks not only have campsites and trailer parks but cabins as well. The state park that I will describe to you is just one of the many that are located all over these United States. It is Gilbert Lake State Park located near a very attractive little community called Laurens in the Catskill Mountains of New York

State. It is a very large state park with three lakes and several ponds. Gilbert Lake is the largest of the three being approximately a mile long. This is the lake where an area is set aside for swimming. All three lakes and the ponds can be fished. There is a recreational area set aside for active sports as well as a playground for young children. The swimming is supervised and there is a small shopping center with limited supplies on the grounds.

The park is open to motor vehicle traffic but only on designated roads for access to the park and campsites and cabins.

It is the rental of one of these cabins that I am going to suggest to the novice camper or the camper who wants to introduce his wife, whether they have a child or not, to the delights of camping.

There are only 30 cabins at Gilbert Lake and they are spaced far enough away from one another so as to give each one more than just a normal sense of privacy. There are two types of cabins available. There is the one bedroom cabin and the two bedroom cabin. They all have a kitchen that contains a gas stove, good sized kitchen sink with running water, (hot water is not provided), overhead kitchen cabinets, refrigerator with a freezer compartment and a broom closet. A straw broom and dust pan are also provided. There is an oversized family room that has a fireplace, (woodburning), picnic-sized table and benches. A single folding bed and an arm chair. The bedrooms all have one double sized bed as well as clothes hanging poles and

shelves. There is also a large screened-in porch with wooden chairs. There is an enclosed flush toilet on the porch.

Outside the cabin is a charcoal grill on a stand and a wood burning fireplace with a grill and a picnic table with benches. An outdoor clothes line is also provided. Clothes washing machines and showers are located in a centralized location a distance from the cabins and are available for use by the tent campers as well as the trailer campers. So here you have rustic living with all of the conveniences of civilization. I have not forgotten that there is no hot water. That is available by keeping a huge pot on the stove filled with water and on a low flame at all times.

How does this help you to break into camping and the true outdoors type of situation? You begin to find out what is is like to cook over an open campfire outside your cabin. That is just one way. You become accustomed to the quiet and the noises of nature by sitting on the screened-in back porch. You learn that the weather is no worse in the country than it is in the city and that the rain drops on the leaves make a louder noise than it does in the city when it hits the pavement. You take hikes through the woods over well marked trails and you will see flowers and trees that you did not know existed. The animals in the woods, deer, raccoon and all the other wildlife will only run away if you approach them too closely. Otherwise you can observe them from a distance and without the use of binoculars.

Besides the swimming, fishing, and hiking there are some organized activities which you can take part in if you so desire. The most exciting is the nature hike which is led by one of the park Rangers. The most interesting part of this hike is when they take you to the valley of fossils. This is an area which is all rock and stone and I defy you to pick any rock off of the ground and not find some fossilized remains. You will even find these fossils outside of your cabin and in the stone in the fireplace inside the cabin. When your stay is over you will go home with an excellent fossil collection and quite possibly start your children on an excellent hobby or career.

The park is one of the most beautiful places to be. Before you end your stay you may well come to believe that you are living in a picture postcard. It is well patrolled by park Rangers whom you will find to be the most courteous people that you have ever met.

There was a time when you could take your dog to Gilbert Lake but that is no longer allowed. I believe that several people abused the privilege by allowing the dog to run lose and several children were bitten. On this point one cannot disagree with the Superintendent of the Park. We only hope that he banned the people who allowed their dogs to roam free. All state and national parks have their rules and regulations and they are handed to every party that enters them. At Gilbert Lake they are framed and hung on the wall near the kitchen door. I have never read any of these rules and regulations in any of our parks that did not make common sense and I cannot find any reason for any person to break them. That is, any REASONABLE PERSON!

You will meet many new people at the park and you will find them to be very friendly. Almost everyone accepts everyone else because they all feel that they have one thing in common that sets them off on the right foot and that is their love for the outdoors. You may even be invited over to someone's trailer or tent to share in hot dogs or hamburgers. This is another way for the novice to see what it is like to live in a trailer or a tent for an extended period of time. The women will begin to talk to one another and your wife will ask certain questions that will be freely answered and in this way she might very well consent to your renting a trailer or tenting outfit for your next vacation or even for a weekend outing before the good weather ends.

These cabins do not cost very much to rent. In 1970 the cost of renting the two bedroom cabin was $56.00 per week. I am sure that in line with everything else this cost has risen too. But even if it has gone to $60.00 or $65.00 per week there is no place else that I know of where you can rent a cabin in an area that has so much to offer for such a low price. All the utilities such as electricity, gas and water are included in that price. The wood for the wood burning fireplace can be purchased from a vendor who has access to the park and he delivers the wood right into your cabin or you can buy it from a store just a few hundred feet from the entrance to the park and transport it to your cabin yourself. The store at the entrance to the park also contains all the necessary foodstuffs you might need during your stay so that if you should run short and not find the article you need in the park store you can get it there along with ice, diapers, baby powder, etc.

In order to become eligible to enter a state park and rent one of the cabins or trailers or tentsites you must make reservations about six months in advance and then it is entered in the lottery. There are so many people who want to take advantage of this inexpensive and beautiful vacation spot that the lottery is the only fair method of distributing the sites. This should not discourage the novice from trying, however because the state park does not ignore your application even if you should lose the lottery. They will inform you almost immediately if your application was not drawn so that you will have plenty of time to make other arrangements.

When you first fill out your application you indicate how long you intend to stay and what week or weeks are most convenient for you and also a second choice of time. If your application is drawn and there is nothing available for the times that you have chosen they will inform you of the dates available so that you can have time to switch vacation dates with someone else at your office if you so desire. A check or money order must accompany your application

which will be refunded to you if your application is not drawn in the lottery or if the dates available are not convenient for you.

I suggest that you try it for one week. I have never met anyone who spent one week in one of the cabins in a state park who didn't regret not making arrangements to spend his entire vacation there before the first week was out. All they could do then was to haunt the admissions cabin hoping that there would be a cancellation. Write to the nearest state park wherever you are and get your application now. They will send it to you and inform you of the dates that they will accept applications. Do not send it in too soon. If it arrives before the date of acceptability it will be returned to you and that will only delay your entrance into the lottery.

MIND YOUR MANNERS

It seems strange, and it really is disturbing, to think that one must devote a section of a book on camping to remind people about common courtesy. It is true that most people practice good manners all of the time but there are enough who only practice good manners part-time or don't practice them at all to make this chapter necessary. In reading this section you will certainly find situations that you have come across that have aggravated you to the point of distraction and you will therefore hope, as we do, that those perpetrators of infractions of good manners will take the hint and mend their ways.

One need only to stop at a roadside picnic table that is littered with the garbage of the previous picnicker. Paper plates, orange peels, soda cans, remnants of all kinds of food are strewn not only on the table but all over the general area. These roadside picnic areas always have plenty of huge disposal cans and yet some people are just too lazy to collect their own refuse and make use of them. Naturally when this happens the place is just swarming with ants and flies. Even if you do cleanup the area of refuse that you did not put there in the first place you cannot enjoy your roadside meal due to all those insects.

To those people who up to this time have felt that a roadside picnic table was an invitation to disorderliness, we respectfully request that they please consider the people who will be coming after them and practice those habits and manners pertaining to neatness and consideration that they expect in their own homes.

At this point we would now like to put in a word for the farmer who is very often the victim of very poor manners on the part of campers and hikers. Many a farmer who would not object to a camper or a hiker using his land has ended up by being a very obstinate hater of all people who come near his pasture. Reason number one is that they enter his property without first asking his permission. Reason number two, and this is probably the most important reason, is that they will very often enter through a gate in his land and will not close it behind them. Now the farmer has to go chasing his cows all over creation to herd them back into his pasture. With all the other work that he has to do he certainly does not appreciate this particular inconsideration.

It is amazing how many people, who would not think of entering anyone else's apartment or house without first knocking on the door or ringing the bell, will nonchalantly open the gate to a pasture and enter that property without first asking permission to do so. There isn't one of these very same people who would dare leave their own living accommodations without closing and locking the door behind them and yet

they will leave the farmer's gate ajar. It is not only ill-mannered to enter someone else's property without his express permission but it is also illegal and it is within the farmer's right to press charges against you for trespassing. If a farmer does give you permission to enter his land, please treat it with the same courtesy that you would grant if you were a guest in his home. Do not litter it, and leave it exactly as you found it so that the farmer will extend his hospitality to the next group of campers and hikers who come along.

One of the most ludicrous sights to see is a group of hikers walking along a trail singing America, The Beautiful as they distribute candy wrappers, soda bottles and apple cores all around them.

When was the last time you saw a young boy poking a snake with a stick while his parents either ignored him or stood by laughing. This scene usually ends with the father crushing the head of the snake with the heel of his boot just to show Junior how brave Daddy is. The snake is usually a harmless garter snake and it was only trying to get away in the first place. This type of action shows a total disregard for all kinds of life and certainly does not benefit anybody and demeans all of mankind.

How about hikers who spread themselves out five abreast when walking along the city sidewalks or crossing bridges? That certainly doesn't show consideration for the other people in the area. These same people always seem to inconvenience other people when they enter public conveyances such as busses or trains as they remove their backpacks. We suggest to these people that when they must pass through the city streets that they either walk single file or no more than two abreast; that they remove their backpacks before they enter the buss or train and hold the packs in front of them so that they do not bang into other people. It would also be nice of you to save your loud singing until you are out on the trail and not annoy the other passengers with loud camp songs and cheers.

If you find it absolutely necessary to take radios, T.V. sets or tape cassette players along on a camping trip, DO NOT PLAY THEM SO THAT THE VOLUME WILL DISTURB NEARBY CAMPERS. When you are out in the forests or the mountains you must remember that sound travels much further than you think it does and raucous music or sporting events can be heard many miles away. It will also spread panic among the wildlife and birds; deer and all other wildlife will exit from the area as quickly as possible if they just don't drop dead from the sound of *some* of the music that is being played today.

If dogs are permitted in the area where you are camping and you take your dog along with you, PLEASE DO NOT ALLOW HIM TO ROAM FREE. It is not only unfair to other campers to have a strange dog come growling around their campsite or messing up the inside of their tent, but it is unfair to the animal. No matter how well-mannered he is with you and the members of your family he might still attack a stranger. If you understand dogs you will understand that he is in a strange place and he thinks that it is his duty to protect you, yours and your property and that any stranger passing by, even a toddler is an enemy. The law in many states is that a dog that attacks a man or a child without provocation must be destroyed. It would be a shame to have the dog destroyed because you would not keep him on a leash.

A baby crying in a nearby campsite at 2 o'clock in the morning can be very annoying. Please remember that the parents of that child would love to have him sleep right on through the night as much as you would. You must also remember that a baby does not cry for no reason at all and therefore you must consider that the child is ill. So please don't start shoutihg to the parents telling them to shut that darned baby up. The noise of the baby is annoying but understandable. The noise of a shouting adult is inexcusable.

People who write their names or poems on the walls of buildings in the city will inevitably do the same with paint on rocks, or in trees with knives when they get out into the country. For some reason beyond my understanding this practice has been dignified by labeling it as GRAFFITI. To me it is pure vandalism and vandalism will never attain any level of respectability in my book of life.

Children with BB guns, pellet guns or CO2 rifles or pistols should never be allowed to roam unsupervised. The massacre of small game and birdlife and the injuries to humans, sometimes permanent, caused by children with these weapons is astronomical. The parents of these children should be held responsible for any infraction of local game and conservation laws as well as for the injuries inflicted on their fellow campers.

Perhaps a check list will help to improve the manners of those people who forget about them.

1. If you cannot improve on the condition of the area at the campsite or picnic ground, at least leave it in the condition in which you would like to find it.

2. Always ask permission before entering private property.

3. Be considerate of the farmer who gives you the privilege of using his property and close any gates you might have opened.

4. Do not walk across any planted fields. Walk around the perimeter or through designated paths.

5. Do not pick fruit, vegetables or flowers on private property.

6. When hiking on trails do not move or damage trail signs or markers. This can lead to confusion and a lost person.

7. Do not in any way mark or deface trees, rocks, fences or walls with knives or paint.

8. You are not the CREATOR so don't be the DESTROYER! Do not kill, harm, bother or needlessly destroy things or creatures that grow in the

open. Why don't you live and HELP LIVE.

CAMPING TRIPS AND PETS

In the preceding chapters we have several times mentioned dogs in context with camping. We have not mentioned cats because it is absolutely ridiculous for anyone to take a cat on a camping trip. The odds are very great that you would never see your little pussy cat again. This is not because it would be killed or kidnapped but because the cats natural curiosity would lead him very far from his owners loving arms. The animal would spy a field mouse or a chipmunk or perhaps some insect in the grass and it would chase it and follow it to it's lair. The little animal might escape but then your cat would spy something else and be off again and with so many delicious birds and little animals to eat he would not even think of returning to you.

The dog is much different. He will usually stay quite close to your campsite and the only reason he might run off is to catch a skunk or a porcupine which was foolish enough to come close to your campsite. Heaven protect us all from a dog that returns from chasing a skunk and pity the poor dog that has gone off chasing a porcupine. If the poor animal does not catch the skunk or porcupine he is sure to pick up a coat full of burrs, ticks, mud and dirt.

You can protect the dog by using tick repellent shampoos and powders and flea repellent dog collars. The dog collars may not be perfect but they certainly do help.

There is no doubt though that you and your dog will both derive great pleasure from your camping trip if you DO NOT take him along. You would be doing him a favor by boarding him at a kennel while you are gone or allowing some loving relative of yours who is just waiting around to inherit your money to take care of him for you.

The rules governing dogs in the states where dogs are permitted in state parks vary from state to state and park to park. In states where dogs are permitted by state law in the parks, you might suddenly find that the park superintendant has placed a restriction on allowing the animal in the park he supervises. So in following lists of states where dogs are permitted in state parks you would be safer if you wrote to the superintendant of the park you wish to go to and find out if he has placed a restriction on dogs in his park.

DOGS ARE NOT PERMITTED TO ENTER THE FOLLOWING STATE'S PARKS:
Delaware, Maryland, Ohio and Pennsylvania.

DOGS ARE PERMITTED IN THE FOLLOWING STATE'S PARKS BUT THEY CANNOT REMAIN OVERNIGHT:
Florida and California.

DOGS ARE PERMITTED IN THE FOLLOWING STATE PARKS BOTH DAY AND NIGHT BUT THEY MUST BE LEASHED CONSTANTLY:
Alabama, Arizona, Arkansas, Connecticut, Massachusetts, Michigan, Minnesota, New Hampshire, New Mexico, New York, South Carolina, Vermont, Washington, Wis-

consin and Wyoming.

No information was available from the remaining states.

Dogs can still be refused admittance to a state park even where there is no regulation against them if you do not have a certificate from a recognized veterinarian stating the most recent dates of rabies innoculation. This should be carried with you at all times.

The following rules and regulations are pretty standard in state parks which permits the entry of dogs.

1. All dogs must be on a leash at all times.
2. The leash must not be over 6 feet long.
3. The dog must be under immediate control at all times.
4. Dogs are not permitted near swimming pools, beaches or lakes.
5. Persons who fail to control their dog will be asked to leave the park.
6. Persons whose dog creates a nuisance or disturbance will be asked to leave the park.
7. Any dog roaming loose will be seized and subjected to the laws of the state pertaining to stray animals.
8. Dogs cannot be left unattended at campsites, picnic tables or other park facilities.
9. The owner of a dog found locked in a car or camping trailer without proper ventilation, food or water will be prosecuted for cruelty to animals.
10. Dog droppings must be disposed of in the following manner. They must be wrapped in paper or foil and placed in trash containers.
11. Dogs must be walked in isolated areas well away from campsites and picnic tables.
12. Owners must show proof of dogs rabies shots before the animal can enter the state park.
13. All dogs in a state park must wear tags certifying that they have been innoculated against rabies.

Don't you agree that Fido would rather stay at home?

KNIVES

As any camper can tell you one of the handiest tools to have around camp is a knife. You can use it to clean a fish, peel an apple or an orange or whittle a point on a stick to hold a hot dog over a fire or to cut a rope or a T-bone steak. A knife has a thousand-and-one uses particularly when you know how to use it and to take care of it.

In my time most boys received their first knife when they were accepted as a tenderfoot boy scout. It was usually presented to them by their father who would then impress upon them the responsibility that was inherent in the ownership of a knife. From that point on it was usually the scoutmaster who taught the boys how to whittle or carve with their new knife.

The ownership of any sharp-edged instrument does carry with it a great deal of responsibility—not only for your own safety, but the safety of your fellow campers. A knife can be a tool, but when it is sticking in your own flesh or that of one of your fellow camp-

For all intents and purposes, this pocketknife is like seven fine tools.

ers it has become a weapon.

Accidents with knives occur when someone is horsing around. Knife throwing is for the experts in the circus and not for a camper who is not familiar with the technique as well as not owning a well balanced throwing knife. The ordinary jackknife or hunting knife when thrown at a tree will very rarely enter the tree blade first. What happens is that some other part of the knife rather than the point of the knife blade will hit the tree causing the knife to bounce off the tree at random and possibly hitting someone standing nearby causing them an injury. There is no excuse for this type of "accident." There is no excuse for using a knife to carve your initials in a tree. This is vandalism. A responsible person learns how to use his tools properly. He also learns how to take care of them and to keep them in excellent working condition.

When a person claims that his knife is so dull it couldn't cut through cream he is admitting that he does not know how to

An example of fine workmanship and handsome design.

take care of his tools.

If you are going to give a knife to a youngster you certainly want him to act responsibly. You might study the list of rules and pass them on to that youngster. You will find them an asset not only in the handling of a knife but any tool.

1. Learn what it is for and learn each part of it.

2. Learn whatever is necessary to keep it in good working order. Oiling, sharpening and cleaning.

3. Learn to be skillful in its use.

4. Learn to use it safely.

5. Learn what to do with it when it is not being used.

6. Learn to make things with it.

There is an old cliche that claims that you can tell a good workman by the way he handles his tools. The saying fits a good camper as well.

There are a great many different kinds of knives. There are butcher knives, butter knives, steak knives, bread knives, but the two kinds of knives that we are most concerned with are the jackknife and the sheath or hunting knife. A jackknife can have one or more blades of varying sizes and shapes that can fold back so that the blade is carried inside the handle. Some jackknives not only have a blade but they also have bottle openers, screwdrivers, corkscrews, can openers and even forks that can fold back into the case. The sheath or hunting knife has just one blade and it cannot be folded back and therefore must be carried in a sheath for safety.

Most jackknives have a ring at one end so that they can be carried on a belt or on a removeable clip that is attached to a belt. The sheath for the hunting knife has a slit through the upper portion through which a belt can slide and hold the sheath at your side ready to carry the knife when it is not being used. Two small strips of leather at the top of the sheath have snaps to hold the knife securely in the sheath.

When kept in good condition the blade or blades of a jackknife will open without any effort at all. One way to keep the blade working freely is to place a drop of machine oil on the hinge and open and shut the blade several times.

Any knife blade can be cleaned by using a drop of oil, or bacon grease, on the blade and then wiping it with a piece of tissue or cloth and steel wool. NEVER try to clean the blade of a knife by rubbing it in sand or dirt. This action will chip the blade.

A sharp knife is a safe knife. A sharp knife when used properly will fulfill its function without causing an injury. A dull knife will not perform properly and can injure the person who is using it.

A knife should be sharpened only on a sharpening stone. Sharpening stones are known by several names. They are called hones, oilstones, whetstones or Carborundum. Any of these stones will provide a grinding surface for your knife. You must remember that they come with varying degrees of coarseness. The coarse stones are used for heavy tools such as hatchets and axes and the fine stones are used to sharpen knives. A drop of oil or several drops of water on the stone will help to reduce the friction when you are working the blade over the stone. When sharpening the blade, you hold the stone with your thumb and forefinger. Make sure that your fingers are below the top and the edge. The knife blade must be held flat on the stone as you move it with a circular motion and applying the pressure away from the knife edge. This action is repeated for the other side of the knife blade.

Twenty to thirty minutes of knife sharpening should give you the edge on the blade that you want. Do not test the sharpness of the blade on your finger. Test it on a piece of wood. A sharp blade has a long thin edge that spreads evenly back to the thickest part of the blade and the marks of the stone will show all across the blade.

If the blade has a nick in it, it can be removed by using a very coarse stone. Tip the blade at an angle along the edge of the stone and keep rubbing until you wear away enough of the edge of the blade along its length to make it an even edge again. Then sharpen it once more on a fine stone.

To open a jackknife you must hold it in both of your hands. You hold the case in your left hand and you grasp the blade between the thumb and index finger of the right hand bending the thumb so that the thumbnail fits into the slot at the top of the blade. Pull the blade out. Keep holding the knife with both hands until the blade is completely open.

To close a jackknife you repeat the action as explained above holding the knife in both hands until the blade is nearly closed. When you feel the tension pulling the blade from between the thumb and index finger you may release the blade. It will then snap shut.

Do not attempt to close a jackknife with one hand or by holding it in one hand and pressing it against your thigh or any other part of your body. Always close it the correct way as described above. Always keep your fingers away from the cutting edge of any knife.

When using any knife you never have the cutting edge of the blade facing your body. The knife should be held firmly by the handle and pushed away from you. Make sure that the area in front and to the side of you is clear before you attempt to whittle or carve. You will be applying a great deal of pressure against the object that you are carving and you can seriously injure anyone standing within the arc of the knife if it should slip.

A knife can cause a great deal of damage when it is not being used. Always close the knife or replace it in its sheath when it is not going to be used. If you must lay it aside for a few moments be sure that it is resting on its side and not on its back. Someone may come along and lean on the cutting edge. Above all do not try to throw it down into the dirt. It is liable to bounce back up and go through your leg or the leg of somebody standing nearby.

THE HAND AXE

The short-handled axe which we are referring to here is used with one hand and usually takes on those jobs that are too clumsy for a long-handled axe. The short-handled axe could be called a work horse because of all the jobs it is called upon to do. Because of the flat top on the opposite end of the cutting edge, it is often called upon to do the work of a hammer. It is an excellent tool and it is inconceivable that anyone would go on a camping trip without one.

As with all tools, it must be used properly to be efficient and it must be handled carefully as it too can be a dangerous weapon. Once again, this tool can be the most dangerous when it is not in use. Naturally when travelling or moving through the woods the axe should be in its sheath which is attached to your belt and hanging at your side. There is usually only one axe at a campsite so the sheath should be removed from your belt and the axe in its sheath should be placed in one designated spot and returned there each time it is not in use.

Many campers will hit the axe into a tree and leave it hanging there until they want it again. This is not only bad for the tree but it can be dangerous for anyone walking by if the axe should drop out of the tree. Another bad habit is to chop it into the ground and let it stay there. Some other camper who is not aware that the axe is there comes walking by and trips over it.

It is safe to hit the cutting edge of the axe into a chopping block

You'll find the Estwing axe useful for many things besides cutting wood—driving tent-stakes for example.

and let it stay there. It can do no one any harm while it is waiting to be used. If you are carrying the axe and it is not in its sheath be sure that you are holding the handle just behind the axe head and that the cutting edge is facing down. When passing the axe to someone else grasp the flat edge of the axe in your hand and point the handle toward them and do not let go until they have a firm grip on it.

When using the axe make sure that no one is standing behind

Whenever possible, use a chopping block like this for cutting stakes.

you or anywhere near the object you are chopping. It is a good idea to announce out loud that you are going to chop some wood, look all around you and make sure that no one is standing within ten feet of you in any direction.

To use the axe properly so that it will work for you most efficiently you must never hold it in the middle of the handle nor very close to the head. You grasp the end of the handle firmly and raise it by arm and wrist motion, allowing the weight of the head to aid

Much firewood is delivered as large logs. Split them into usable size with an Estwing pick and a wedge.

in bringing it down in place. Your blows should be sharp, steady and firm. Pecking, quick blows will be ineffective.

Make sure that you are standing in such a way that you will not injure your legs or any other part of your body should you strike a glancing blow or the axe misses the object you are working on.

THE LONG-HANDLED AXE

The long-handled axe is used mainly for chopping long logs to a size that will fit the fireplace. There was a time it was used for chopping down trees but we hope that no one is doing that anymore unless they are dead trees.

If you adhere to the following basic rules when using the long handled axe, you should never have any problems.

1. The log to be cut should be placed on the ground.
2. If the log is not heavy enough to stay still, it is best to place four heavy rocks, one on each side at one end and one on each side at the other end, to steady it. Pegs driven in at these four points will prove to be more effective.
3. The axe should be held easily in both hands. Right handed people should hold the axe with the right palm under the handle near the head and the left palm over the handle at the end. Reverse this procedure if you are lefthanded.
4. Stand facing the log. Place the head of the axe on the log. Step back from the log leaving the head of the axe on the log and have both hands at the back of the handle. With your arms outstretched you should be within easy reaching distance of the log.
5. Spread your feet apart so that your weight is evenly distributed.
6. Check overhead and on all sides to see that there are no overhanging branches that will interfere with the swing of the axe.
7. To make sure that the distance between you and the log is correct, let the axe fall lightly on the log a couple of times.
8. You are now ready to chop the log. As you get into the swing of it you will develop a nice steady rhythm that will keep you from tiring too quickly.

SAFETY! SAFETY! SAFETY! Your feet must be spread apart at all times so that if you should miss the log with the axe it will go between your legs and not injure you. Never take your eyes off of the spot on the log that you want to strike. If you happen to be looking at your foot when the axe is on the down swing the odds are that you will hit your foot.

AXE SHARPENING

This is a very simple procedure. Place the flat head of the axe in the palm of your left hand and grasp it tightly. Hold a coarse sharpening stone in your right hand and place it flat against the blade. Keeping it flat move the stone in a circular motion against the edge. Turn the axe and repeat this procedure on the other side of the blade. Don't forget to use some water or oil to reduce the friction. ●

CHAPTER 10

SIT DOWN, YOU'RE ROCKING THE BOAT

Camping is a safe recreational activity, but as in all things, carelessness can lead to disaster. A word to the wise is sufficient . . . be wary when on the water.

■ If you were to go to the boat show you would come away with the idea that Americans must own as many boats as they do cars. This is not a fact now but it may be a fact in the not too distant future. They have displays of boats that cover every category from rubber rafts to luxury yachts. Yes, Americans seem to be overwhelmed with a passion for boating and if each and every manufacturer represented at shows can sell enough boats to stay in business then our waterways will literally be jammed with pleasure boats of every description.

If boats are so popular then it stands to reason that boat camping is on the increase as well. Boat camping is when you spend your days on the water and nights on the shore or water. The experienced boat camper is not only familiar with the art of campcraft but watercraft as well.

The backpacker and recreational vehicle enthusiasts have limitations that the boat camper is not handicapped with. The boat camper can reach campsites that are inaccessible to his landbound brethren. I have had boat campers tell me that if they had the time they would be able to float themselves clear across the United States without ever having to cross the land. Boat campers claim that they can make camp in the evening along some shores that have never felt the foot of a tourist or the polluter. They also claim that of all the camping enthusiasts they are the most efficient since they travel longer distances with a limited amount of space for food and equipment. This point may be debatable and it is not one that we will take up here.

Canoeing, sailing and powerboating are the three basic types of water transportation. The one best suited for the boat camping enthusiast is canoeing because it gives him access to wilderness waterways that would be inpenetrable with a sailing boat or power boat. The sailboat depends on the wind and strong current. Small power boats may have the mobility of a canoe but they are not as maneuverable. Powerboat enthusiasts will argue this point and they are always stopped when asked which boat they would rather be in when they must maneuver through rapids? The answer every time is a canoe. Powerboats are also polluters. I am not just referring to the oil scum that is left on the clear water when they pass through. I am referring to the noise they bring into the quiet back country.

The canoe has an undeserved reputation for instability. It is actually as safe as a rowboat and much easier to handle. You don't have to be an expert to handle a canoe. A little knowledge, and a little practice and you can get where you want to go and enjoy yourself at the same time. The motor-driven boat makes so much noise on these back country waterways that any wildlife that might be along the shore will have disappeared in fright long before you even get near them. Watching deer and small game along the shoreline is part of the pleasure one gets when he is moving along the water in a canoe. He arrives every-

A canoe-run down white-water is a thrill to be long-remembered. But make sure you load your gear properly and maintain correct paddling positions.

where unannounced and by the time the animals are aware of his presence the man or men in the canoe have usually watched them and are already passing on.

The boat camper who is going off on his first canoe trip should remember that paddling is physical labor. He is going to be applying constant pressure on his arms, back and legs so he should not attempt to set any speed or distance records on the first day out. Make the first day on the water short and slow and be sure to start the trip in fairly calm, if not placid, water.

Once again the novice is advised not to buy a canoe when he is making his first trip. It is best to rent it. Naturally if you have gone on several boatcamping trips with a friend and you are familiar with the handling of a canoe this warning is needless.

Whether you rent or buy your first canoe we advise that you look for stability rather than speed. For the two man boatcamping trip the recommended canoe size is 18 feet long with a beam width of 36 inches and a midships depth of 13 inches. The canoe that tapers sharply from amidship to stern or bow is built for speed. The canoe that is built for speed suffers a loss of stability. The novice will find this one very hard to handle as it rides low and hard into waves instead of gliding gently over them. Besides, you are not going to the races you are going on a camping trip and you don't have to knock yourself out getting anywhere. The canoe that you rent or buy should be a little heavier in the belly and flatter on the bottom. This not only makes for easier handling but gives you more space for your gear. It will also ride higher in the water even if it is loaded to the gunwales. A boat with the measurements mentioned will not only hold two men very comfortably but it will carry many hundreds of pounds of equipment and still remain stable in almost any kind of weather.

What kinds of materials are canoes made of and which one is the best? We can answer the first question but you will have to decide the answer to the second one for yourself. There are three kinds of materials used in the manufacture of canoes.

1. Wood with a canvas covering.
2. Aluminum.
3. Fiber glass.

The wood and canvas covered canoe is the one that was used by the Indians and our pioneering forefathers. It is still the favorite of most backwoods guides. It moves through the water very quietly and it is a very stable craft. It weighs no more than the modern aluminum canoe and is efficient when you are paddling into the wind. The one drawback with the wooden canoe is that it takes a lot of Tender Loving Care. Every year before putting it back in the water you must refinish and patch it to prevent the absorption of moisure. The inside must also be varnished. You must also be very careful when you are on the water so that you don't hit rocks or sharp surfaces. Those obstructions that would just glance off of an aluminum or fiberglass canoe could slash the canvas or take a rib or piece of planking out of your wooden canoe. Repair kits are standard equipment for all boatcamping trips. For the canvas and wood canoe the patch kit should contain Ambroid glue, un-bleached muslin patches and sand-paper so that you can rough up the edges to help the glue make a bond.

The aluminum canoe is light and rugged and does not require the care of the wood/canvas canoe. It doesn't rust, rot, or ab-sorb moisture. It never needs painting, caulking, or refinishing. It can be punctured but it takes a lot to do it. You will probably end up with more dents and it is possible to live with those. What are its drawbacks? The first is that it is infernally noisy. Even in calm water it won't remain silent. On a choppy day it can sound like a bunch of kids beating on their mother's aluminum pots. If you are in the canoe and a sudden spring or fall shower should come upon you, you will suddenly feel as though you are paddling a floating block of ice. If it is on shore and turned over it very quickly becomes a reflector oven and can give you a nasty blister if you touch it. Aluminum canoes are very buoyant and can be diffi-cult to handle in a fresh wind. This is a particular problem when they are not fully loaded. The craft is extremely buoyant and if it capsizes it can be righted very easily. Once it is righted it has the

Two beautiful examples of fiberglass canoes, well-manned and correctly balanced.

nasty habit of taking off in the slightest breeze and you could be left floundering in the water. This is a problem because the cardinal rule when a boat capsizes is that you should hang onto it and not try to swim for shore. With an aluminum canoe you must grab it and never let go of it. If the canoe has capsized and you were able to hold onto it after it righted you will have a problem getting back into it if there is the slightest breeze or current. When renting or purchasing any metal canoe insist on the model that has styrofoam flotation chambers. Air pockets can flood if the canoe is punctured. Patching material for aluminum canoes is Liquid Solder.

Fiberglass canoes have a distinct disadvantage because of their weight. If a fiberglass canoe is manufactured to come in at the same weight as a wood or aluminum canoe then the manufacturer made a canoe that is shallow amidship and narrow in the beam. This will give you less stability and less room for your gear. A fiberglass canoe built to the standard 18 foot length will weigh in from ten to fifteen pounds heavier than either the wooden or the aluminum canoe. It is durable, sturdy, weather resistant and will keep its head in the wind. The patch kit for the fiberglass canoe will contain an epoxy-resin glue. Chewing gum and spruce pitch can be used for temporary repairs of small leaks.

PADDLING

How do you paddle a canoe? Should you use a long-handled paddle or a short-handled paddle? Is a narrow blade better than a wide blade? We will try to answer

101

these questions for you but in the long run it is a decision that you will have to make for yourself and you can only make that decision after you have had some experience.

As we said earlier, there is a great deal of strain placed on the arm, shoulder, back and neck muscles. This comes from the resistance of the water against the blade of the paddle. After a short time on the water a novice may get the feeling that he is paddling through mud. The novice can alleviate this feeling to a degree by using a paddle that is made of light but resilient wood. The lightest paddles are those made of spruce and I don't care if you are a professional football player, if you have never paddled a canoe before it is best for you to start with this paddle. Maple and ash also make good paddle materials. Maple is the heavier of the two. Ash is easier to pull through the water.

Do not take the length of the paddle lightly. It is very important. How do you determine the efficient length of the paddle? That depends on where you will be sitting in the canoe. The man riding in the bow (front) of the canoe should be sure that his paddle reaches from his toe to his chin when he is in a standing position. The man who will be paddling from the stern (rear) of the canoe needs a paddle which will give him more bite in the water. His paddle should reach from his toe to his eye when he is in a standing position. This holds even if you are over six feet tall. Short persons should use an extra

long paddle so that they do not have to constantly bend over when they are paddling from an upright position. The constant bending when upright can not only tire you out very quickly but it can actually knot the muscles of the stomach and cause a great deal of discomfort. The extra length of the paddle will give you deeper immersion which will give you a much quieter stroke.

Which is best, the wide blade or narrow blade? You get an easier draw with a narrow blade and there is less exertion. The wider blade bites deeper which adds speed and distance with each stroke. But it does demand more exertion. Since the novice should be more concerned with stamina than speed it is my opinion that he should use the narrow blade.

The paddle should never be used as a pole or a shovel or any of the other things that people try to do with them. This will chip, crack or break the blade which should always be thin and sharp on the edge. Copper stripping can be tacked around the edge to protect it.

There are various techniques for paddling a canoe but under certain situations there will be no disagreement. When a canoe is not carrying a load and you are the lone paddler you must kneel amidships and slightly toward the stern. This can be a very uncomfortable position which can give you leg cramps and bruised knees. Practice is the only thing that will help you get rid of the leg cramps and get used to the position. A foam rubber pad under the knees will avoid bruises there. This just

It is possible to paddle long
distances without tiring.

happens to be the most efficient way for a lone paddler to paddle an empty canoe. If you sit in the stern of the boat the bow will come up out of the water like a speedboat and the canoe become unmanageable. Start out by doing it the right way even if it is more arduous in the beginning. You will finally become accustomed to it and you will never want to do it any other way.

When there are two paddlers, the more experienced man should take the stern position. He will not only steer the canoe from this position but he can keep an eye on the load as well as the less experienced man in the bow. The choice of using the seats or paddling from a kneeling position is up to you when there are two men in the canoe. Some experienced canoeists will use the seats at all times except when the weather is bad. Then they drop to their knees thereby lessening the wind resistance and adding to the speed. Others like to paddle from a kneeling position at all times believing that it lowers the center of gravity.

STROKES

1. CRUISING STROKE: This is the basic stroke that moves the canoe forward in a straight line. The paddle is drawn through the water parallel to the keel. The two man cruise stroke is as follows: The man in the stern draws away from the gunwale and the man in the bow draws toward the gunwale.

2. PITCH STROKE: Very effective and easy on the paddler.

As the paddle passes the canoers hip line it is feathered. This means to turn the paddle on its edge. Then draw it back and hold for just a moment. Withdraw it from the water and continue to repeat the motion.

3. THE INDIAN OR UNDERWATER STROKE: This is truly silent paddling because the paddle never leaves the water. After drawing the paddle back, the blade is feathered back to its original position under water.

4. REVERSE SWEEP: This stroke is used to turn the canoe around. This is done by placing the paddle in the water and pushing forward rather than pulling it backward.

5. HOLDING STROKE OR JAM: This stroke will slow the canoe down. It is accomplished by dropping the blade into the water perpendicular to the canoe and holding it there.

There are strokes for maneuvering a canoe in fast water of running rapids but it is recommended that the novice not try either of these waters until he has mastered the basics of canoeing.

Swift shallow streams and rapids can be negotiated very effectively with the technique known as poling. We do not recommend that any novice attempt poling in any fast waters but instead he can begin to practice the technique in shallow and quiet waters.

Since the pole must be at least fourteen feet long you will have to stand up in the canoe. This is supposed to be breaking the very first rule that you learned which is never to stand up in a boat. If you can figure out a way to handle a fourteen foot pole in a canoe without standing up I would appreciate it if you would send me the information. The most difficult part of poling is learning to keep your balance while standing in the canoe. You will probably take a few dunkings the first few times and that is why we suggest that you begin by practicing in shallow and quiet water. The poler must stand at the stern of the canoe. If you do not have another person sitting in the bow then you will have to use ballast. If you don't, the bow of the canoe will raise up out of the water and you will have absolutely no control. Until you feel comfortable in the canoe while standing up do not attempt to do any poling. Get the feel of the balance of the pole by holding it and just floating around near the shore line.

Poles are made of hickory, ash or maple. The best one is hickory since it is the hardest wood. An iron shoe at the bottom of the pole will prevent the pole from splintering and will give you better gripping power.

Place the pole over the side of the canoe and let it slide into the water. Apply pressure downward and backward letting your hands move over one another just as though you were climbing a rope. When you reach the top of the pole you crouch slightly and push off. Remember not to let go of the pole. Take it with you. This crouching and pushing off action will send you off like a shot so be careful that the canoe doesn't shoot out from under you.

A canoe can be slowed down when poling. The technique is known as SNUBBING. You place the pole in the water close to the gunwale, lean and apply pressure forward. The amount of snubbing you will have to do depends on how fast the canoe is moving. It is a good idea to wear gloves when poling as you can work up some very uncomfortable blisters.

With a little practice on your part you should be able to handle a canoe in no time at all. That includes poling as well. Don't be discouraged if you should wind up in the drink the first couple of times. Just hang in there and you will soon be having some of the most exciting times of your life.

PACKING THE CANOE

Packing the canoe is very simple. All you have to remember is that the heaviest items go on the bottom. An experienced camper will always save one heavy piece of gear to go in last. This will help to adjust the balance after the canoe is loaded so that you don't have to be shifting the load over and over again. Never lash the gear into a canoe. An upset canoe, even when it is full of water can support its passengers but not when the gear is lashed and held on board. It is wise to lash one extra paddle in the canoe for emergencies.

A bailing can and a large sponge should be part of your standard canoe equipment. They will not only keep the bottom dry but even half an inch of water in a canoe can shift its balance.

A WORD TO THE WISE

Waves and white water are difficult enough for the experts so we certainly don't recommend that the novice attempt to do battle with these elements. The novice may start out on a nice clear day when the water is as calm and smooth as a sheet of glass. Suddenly, without any warning a stiff wind begins to blow and this calm and beautiful lake begins to act like the ocean in a hurricane. He is now fighting four foot waves, storm-tossed white caps and a very fast current. If the lake is big enough this is actually what can occur. What can you do if you are caught in a situation like this?

You must get out of harms way and the easiest way to do that is to head toward the lee shore. The lee shore is the direction opposite the wind. Once there, you can paddle in the shallows until you can land the boat.

If you are in the middle of the lake when this situation occurs, or nearer to the windward shore, do not turn the stern of the canoe toward the wind and head leeward. If you are not kneeling in the boat you must do so at once. Do not point the bow of the canoe into the waves. Or you may let them hit you broadside. You will be taken off course by these waves so you will have to make a course correction by turning sharply in the opposite "tack" or direction. There is no way to avoid going in a zigzag pattern, and this will make strenuous physical demands on you that will have your muscles aching long before you reach safety. But you will reach safety—all out of breath and muscle bound. The roughness of the weather should in no way affect your stroke. It must remain smooth and rhythmic. The only time you don't paddle is when you are taking a wave or if you see that you are not making any headway.

Never for any reason whatsoever travel by canoe under storm conditions. If the weather is just windy and drizzly and you must travel then it is best to travel by night as the winds usually drop after sundown. Natural light or a flashlight should give you enough visibility to make fairly good time.

Rapids are caused by underwater rocks and obstructions. You will usually see and hear them long before you get to them. When you do, it is best to head for the shore. The only people I have ever seen brave the rapids in a canoe are Hollywood stuntmen. There are some canoeists who claim that they know how to ride the rapids and they have all kinds of suggestions as to how to do it. I will not pass on this information to you as I do not know how reliable it really is. I will tell you to do what the Indians did with their fully laden canoes. They took their canoes out of the water and "portaged" or hiked their way around the rapids. If they thought that was the best way to brave the rapids I would suggest that you follow their example.

PORTAGING

Canoe or lightboat campers never pitch their camps very far from shore. They will only have to pack their gear a few hundred feet but don't forget that along with that gear is a 50 or 60 pound canoe. You can be sure that they will not get too far away from the water with that load.

A two man trip should only necessitate the use of two packs. Since you will not be carrying them very far you will stuff as much gear into them as you can get. The Duluth pack (described in a previous chapter) is the best for jamming in a lot of gear and a pack basket (described in a previous chapter) is the best choice for food and cooking utensils. Do not pack food and cooking supplies in the gear pack and vice versa. There is a very good reason for this. Once you get to your campsite the person carrying the gear pack will begin to set up the camp and the person carrying the food pack will begin to prepare the food. In this way it doesn't take very long for the camp to be set up nor for both parties to sit down and eat. Believe me after a day of paddling a canoe you are both going to be very hungry and you will not want to wait very long for a meal.

The national parks and other public camping areas have clearly marked portage trails from the shore to the campsite. If there are no signs you can locate a trail by debarking on level terrain and following signs that might have been left there by previous campers. If you insist on being a trail blazer always land your canoe in a flat level area with very little vegetation. Lugging a canoe and backpacks over weeds and hills is no picnic.

The job of portaging can be simple if certain basic instructions are followed.

Carrying two backpacks and a canoe even a few hundred feet may seem like a Herculian feat to many of you city dwellers but the human body can handle a great deal more than that if it becomes absolutely necessary. You may even think that it is impossible for a man to handle a bulky 50 or 60 pound canoe by himself but he can do it. I have seen some men carry the canoe and the small backpack of food at the same time. If the man carrying the canoe finds that is all he can comfortably carry then the other camper hooks the pack basket on his shoulders and places the Duluth pack on top of that.

Carrying the canoe does not really present a problem as commercial yokes with shoulder pads are now on the market. Some boat campers even make their own. So carrying the canoe can be done very comfortably once you get it on your shoulders. Getting it on your shoulders is the diffi-

A portage over rough terrain is best done with rugged, lightweight equipment.

cult part.

The canoe must be out of the water and up on dry land. The interior of the canoe is turned away from you. You bend over and grab the center thwart as low as you can. The next two motions must be accomplished simultaneously. You thrust your knees against the bottom of the boat and pull up on the center thwart just as though you intended to throw the canoe over your shoulders. If this action is properly coordinated you will find the canoe up over your head and settling down comfortably on your shoulders. Now you can start walking. You will have to tilt the bow up slightly so that you will be able to see where you are going. Take long measured strides. Do not bounce, mince or take short steps.

If the gear is just too heavy to be carried in one trip then the campers will have to make two trips. One trip to carry the gear and one trip to carry the canoe. Most boatcampers seem to agree that it is easier for one man to carry the canoe than for two.

They say it doesn't jiggle as much when one man is carrying it and that synchronization of stride as well as direction can sometimes be very difficult when approaching the campsite.

When making camp, don't forget to either weight or tie the canoe down. A brisk wind might blow up while you are sleeping and your canoe will take off like a kite and either be damaged or fly off into the next state and you might never know it until you awaken the next morning.

CAR TOPPERS FOR CARRYING CANOES

Learn how to tie the canoe down to the top of your car in a proper manner. Tieing the canoe to the car topper is not enough. The canoe must also be secured to the car as well. If you don't tie the canoe to the car it will begin to spin around like the rotor on a helicopter.

The proper way to make use of the car topper is as follows. The canoe must be lashed tightly to the topper so that it will not sway from side to side. The front and back ends are then lashed securely to the front and back bumpers with nylon line or a strong rope. There must be absolutely no play in the load. If you are driving and you see that the lines are becoming slack or you can hear it sliding around on the top, stop the car at once and retie all the lines. Just think about the damage a flying canoe can do on one of our super highways. It has happened several times with very tragic results.

There is no argument that the larger power boats are very beauti-ful. Some of them have galleys and sleeping quarters and you can spend your nights as well as days on board. I feel that they are limited since they must be used on the larger lakes and cannot be maneuvered into the smaller backwoods streams.

The smaller sailing vessels have a little more entree into the shallower waters but they too have their limitations since they must rely on the wind for movement therefore the canoe is just not the old standby but an essential craft for any backwoods boatcamper. You can put a sailing rig on it. With a mainsail and a jib it is transformed into one of the hottest sailing crafts you will ever handle. This is not recommended for a beginner nor is it something that a boatcamper wants to carry along on his trip. It is just too much extra gear to carry. It doesn't take too much work to adapt a canoe so that it can accommodate a three or five horsepower motor. But most motors are powered by gasoline and if the boatcamper is ecology minded which most of them are, then he will not want to pollute the backwoods waters. Once again the motor becomes extra gear to carry on portages as do gasoline and oil. Electric motors for canoes seem to be the coming thing in reservoirs where gasoline engines are prohibited. They can run for about 12 hours on a charge from a 12 volt battery. They run silent, they give off no smell and they do not leave behind a coating of oil on the water. They are somewhat more expensive than gasoline motors but over the long run you can make up the difference in cost by the savings on gasoline.

The square sterned guide canoe can be used with or without a motor. It is larger and broader than the standard canoe and it gives you more stability and depth. The drawback with this canoe is that it weighs about 115 pounds without the motor and that could really give you a problem on a portage. So with all the doo-dads and gimmicks that come along with progress the man who wants to go on backwoods camping trips must rely on the canoe that still has the same basic design as the one that was used by the American Indian long before the European ever set foot on these shores.

BACKWOODS CAMPING

One of the most annoying problems that boat campers encounter are wind and insects. As you hit the shoreline the insects will descend on you like relatives who have just heard that you won the lottery. Strong winds can blow the camp down or keep you awake all night by snapping the canvas of your tent. This will occur if you set your camp up too close to the water. Those signs that mark the portage trails in our national parks will take you directly to good camping areas. If you are blazing your own trail to a camping area you must use the same discretion in choosing your campsite as you would if you were making camp in the backwoods. That is high ground, etc. If you have no choice except to camp along the shore get as far back from the water as you can.

Do not set up or try to make camp anywhere near heavily weeded shorelines. Just before sundown clouds of bugs will rise up out of those weed and they will be so thick that they can actually blot out the sun.

Use some thought when you set up your fireplace. If it is between the water and the camp it will not only blow ashes all over the camp but the smoke will be blowing directly into the tent. Set the fireplace off to the side and if possible in the back of the tent.

Don't attempt to burn driftwood from pilings or wood from abandoned piers. The possibility that it was chemically waterproofed is very high. This will make it burn fast, hot and smelly. There is no doubt that it will spoil the taste of the food.

You can lighten your load by taking along a quickie camping tarp rig in place of a tent. The canoe can serve as a ridge pole and you can lash the end of the tarp to stakes driven into the ground. The tarp can also be used for a lean-to by stripping four saplings and lash them around the four edges of the tarp. Take two upright forked sticks and drive them into the ground. Lift up one end of the tarp and rest the two extended ends into the forks. Now you have a sturdy lean-to.

The tarp can also make an A-tent. Stretch the tarp over a pole or rope between two uprights. Drive stakes into the ground and lash the loose edges of the tarp to the stakes. The quickie camping tarp rig is very popular with boat campers as it eliminates the carrying of tent poles, which, as light as they are, still add extra weight.

BEACH CAMPING

The biggest problem the beach camper has is getting his boat out of the water. Flies can be as big a problem to the beach camper as they are to the boatcamper if he is not selective in choosing his campsite. There are plenty of places along the ocean that are free of flies and if the beach camper is in an area where he is bothered by them it is his own fault.

Now we get back to the main problem of beaching and mooring the boat so that it won't be swamped during the night. Beaching the boat becomes a ticklish chore as the boat must be edged in to shore very slowly cutting the engines and lifting the props out of the water just before they scrape bottom. You can't wait until you feel the props scrape the bottom as they might hit a rock which could damage them. You should have enough forward motion for the boat to drift into shore. If you don't, you can push the boat in with a pole. It will take some work to get the boat all the way up on the beach even if the waves are very slight. A minor ripple seems to be a tidal wave when you are standing on the deck. If you had some round logs you could use them as rollers to get the boat ashore but it is impractical to carry a cord of wood on a boat. If you are lucky you

A well set-up beach location is one of the more pleasant aspects of camping.

might find some slippery drift-wood along the beach that could be used for this purpose but the odds are that you will have to use raw muscle to gain your objective.

Everyone gets off the boat. A line is tied to the bow. Now everyone pushes and pulls. People pushing on the side of the boat had best watch their feet. A sudden shifting in the boats movement can inflict some very painful injuries to the toes. Now that you have the boat on the beach the anchor should be tied to the bowline and the bowline tied to something stationary and solid. The best time to beach a boat is at high tide. This way you won't have to worry about the boat or your camp being floated during the night. If you cannot get the stern out of the water you must have a well secured bowline and your anchor attached to a stern-line.

SAIL CAMPERS

The people who man the sail-boats very rarely do any camping ashore. Although their sailboat is lighter than the motor boat they have a problem with the extended keel that is under the boat. So they will pull into a cove that is protected from the wind and drop their sails. A small mountaineers tent is set up on deck and a small butane or propane stove cooks their meal. Tucked away in a sleeping bag inside their little tent with the cool ocean breeze blowing across the deck they are gently rocked to sleep by the waves. Of course a sudden storm might give them a rude awakening—but that is the life of a sailor—O.

BOAT CAMPING SAFETY RULES

One of our main objectives in this manual is to try and make your stay in the great outdoors a safe one. We tell you how to set up your camp, start your fires and handle your tools in a correct manner so as to prevent you from injuring yourself and others.

You may feel that this constant emphasis on safety is redundant and that is possibly annoying to you. If this is true then we do apologize to you but we will not mend our ways because your well-being and the well-being of the members of your party is too important for us to be discouraged by that attitude.

A man going into the wilderness country, whether he is in a recreational vehicle, on foot, horse or in a canoe, who is not safety conscious is asking for trouble.

We will continue to press our point and hope that we can reach as many people as possible because each person that we convince to be prepared for emergencies means several people who will not be injured, in pain, or dead.

1. LIFE JACKETS OR FLOATING SEAT CUSHIONS:
Either one or both should be standard equipment aboard anything that floats. It is not uncommon on boats where children or toddlers are on board to see these youngsters walking around on deck wearing their life jackets. This is an excellent idea. The only problem is that the life jackets worn by the children are, in very

many cases, the only life jackets on board that boat. It will not help the child to be the only one wearing a life jacket if all the adults on board drown for the lack of one. There should be a life jacket available for every person aboard the boat and they should be aware of where the life jackets are stowed. Persons in canoes, whether on small lakes or backwoods camping trips should wear their life jackets all the time they are in the canoe. If the canoe should capsize your only concern should be to get back into it and not floundering around in the water trying to stay afloat while you look around for the life jacket. It is a rare day that you don't see someone entering a boat carrying a pillow or an inflatable doughnut. This is because the seats on most boats are not padded. It would be a good idea for the owner of the boat to have floating seat cushions as an extra precaution. Even if they are never used in an emergency the owner and his guests will always be assured of comfort. In some areas where the law demands that the Coast Guard or some other local government agency issue licenses for boats they will not be issued if life jackets are not part of the standard equipment of the boat. This law should be adopted by every one of the United States.

2. FIRST AID KIT:
Every boat, no matter what size, should have a first aid kit

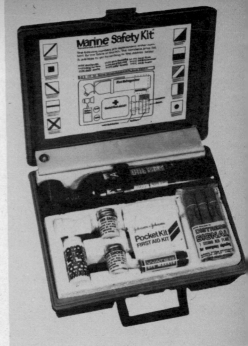

An excellent example of a compact marine first aid and safety kit.

as part of its standard equipment. They do come in waterproof flotation packages. The contents should be checked periodically for expiration dates and replaced if necessary.

3. RADIOS:
Almost all of the ocean going pleasure power boats come equipped with two-way radios or ship-to-shore telephones. These boats also sail on the Great Lakes. The owners of smaller power boats who, for reasons of economy, did not have a two-way radio included in the boat that they purchased should investigate the C.B. radio. The C.B. (citizens band) unit is a two way radio that

can be purchased, depending on the size of the unit, very inexpensively. There are small units that can operate on flashlight batteries or they can be adapted to work from your boats power supply. The unit contains a transmitter and a receiver as well as a microphone that can be hand-held or one that is built right into the radio. Licenses for the C.B. radios can be obtained for a small fee from the Federal Communications Commission, Washington, D.C. Some small boats have only short wave receivers which are tuned in on the wave-length used by the U.S. Coast Guard which broadcasts weather reports at specific times day and night. Smaller craft should all be equipped with small transistor radios and tuned to a station that gives local weather reports. There are some radio stations that broadcast weather reports every 15 or 20 minutes. Any one of these radios can keep the boat camper whether he is in a canoe in the backwoods, in a power boat on a lake or a pleasure boat on the ocean, aware of any sudden changes in the weather so that he can act accordingly.

4. METEOROLOGY:

It would be a good idea for all campers to have some knowledge of meteorology but it really should be a must for all boat owners and particularly for boat campers. Where boat licenses are required, a short course in meteorology is given by the U.S. Coast Guard or the issuing agency. Adult education courses in many communities include it in their cirriculum. My eleven year old son took and passed the course at a mini-semester given at his school. The course may not make you eligible to become a Television Weather Reporter but it will give you enough information on cloud formations and climatic conditions to know when puffy cumulus clouds are forming and becoming gray and ragged around the edges and that caution should be exercised on a hot, hazy, windless day. Boat campers should be hyper-sensitive to wind conditions and learn as much about them as they can.

5. FIRE EXTINGUISHER:

Another item that should be standard equipment on all boats even in the canoe of the backwoods boat camper. We don't believe there is any reason to worry about a canoe bursting into flames while it is in the water but it could come in handy while you are in camp. It is necessary on all power boats because of the presence of gasoline. Also the possibility of cooking fires starting in the galley.

6. BOAT LOADING:

Loading a boat is neither an art nor a science. It is just common sense. Do not overload your boat with gear or people. An overloaded boat is easily capsized. The load must be evenly balanced and distributed.

7. SWIMMING:

It is inconceivable to think that anyone would go out on a boat without at least a rudimentary knowledge of how to stay afloat in the water. Yet every year we read about tragedies occuring on boat trips because someone did not know how to swim. Swimming courses are available through Adult Education courses in some communities. The Y.M.C.A. always has a notice pasted on its bulletin board announcing swimming classes for beginners and the Red Cross is a leading advocate of swimming for everyone. Life-saving techniques are also taught by the above named organizations. Everyone should know how to give artificial respiration in case of a swimming accident. A life can be saved if you have the knowledge to restore the breathing of a person who has been involved in a swimming accident. As delightful as water may be, it can also be very dangerous. You must always be very respectful of it. Diving into an unknown stream can lead to a fractured skull or a broken neck. The best swimmer in a party should first check the bottom for depth, rocks, holes and drop-offs. Never swim alone. Dependence on inflated tubes or air mattresses is foolhardy. A slow leak or a chance puncture could leave you stranded in deep water without support and six feet of water is as dangerous as sixty feet if it is over your head. You may not be aware of the hazardous undertows or tidal currents until you are being swept out to sea. Then it is too late. You can be surprised by deceptively swift currents in river and streams also. The waters in some mountain areas could be so cold that they could put you in a state of shock and you could drown before any member of your party realized what was happening.

8. WATER PUMPS:

Large power craft usually come equipped with bilge pumps or hand pumps that can be utilized to empty the boat of water in case it is swamped. Smaller craft should all be equipped with bailing buckets.

9. NAUTICAL RULES AND REGULATIONS:

Do not attempt to operate a power boat or go out in a power boat unless you are familiar with, or the operator of that craft is familiar with, the nautical rules and regulations. The U.S. Power Squadron has classes in every major city in the United States. Some states will not issue boat licenses unless the operator has taken this course. This course not only teaches you how to read nautical maps it also informs you of the traffic regulations of the waterways as well as a basic mechanics course.

CAPSIZING AND FLOODING:

Do not panic and try to swim to shore if your boat should capsize or flood. Remain with the boat until help arrives. Almost all modern boats, even those made of metal or fiber-glass, have flotation that will keep them afloat. You can climb onto it or hang onto it and it will keep you afloat, too.

RENT OR BUY

The main consideration as to whether you should rent a boat or buy a boat is always financial. The secondary consideration is where you will store that boat if you do buy it. Whether it is a canoe or a power boat it is going to cost you money. The original purchase price does not end the money that you are going to have to spend on that craft. You must consider the cost of insurance and maintenance as well. Where do you keep that boat when it is not in use? Larger power craft will have to pay for mooring rights. Suburban dwellers can keep their smaller power boat in their garage or yard. This necessitates the purchase of a trailer. The apartment dweller does not even have that option of keeping his boat, whether power or canoe, in a yard or garage. He must pay for storage the year round. In the long run, unless you are very rich, it would seem wiser for you to rent your boat. This includes the canoe. Almost all recreational areas that are around water have canoes available for rental. No matter what the cost of rental you will save money over the long run by not having to buy a topper for transportatioor the additional cost of storage. The power boat owner should sit down and add up the costs he has to pay for his boat. Start with the original purchase price then add on the cost of insurance, trailer, (if boat is kept on his own property) or mooring privileges. Do not forget the cost of maintenance. Now he should add up the amount of time he actually makes use of that boat over the year. He should total up both figures. Then investigate the cost of renting a boat and he might find out that he would save money by renting a power boat. Usually a larger and more modern boat can be rented over a period of years for less money than it costs to own one. You must consider the fact that when you own a boat it costs you money whether you use it or not. When you rent a boat you are only paying for it when you are using it. It must be obvious that I advocate the rental of boats. I think it is very practical.

BOATGROUNDS AND MARINAS

With more than 23,000 miles of inland and inter-coastal waters that can be navigated by small craft, the combination of cruising and camping is becoming more popular every day. It is possible to cruise the entire East Coast to Florida along an almost fully protected route. Cruising the Gulf Coast to the Mexican border is also very popular. Boatgrounds and shoreside camping areas can be found on all recreational waterways supervised by the government. Most government campgrounds on the waterways have outboard motor launching facilities as well as recreational facilities. The U.S. Army Corps of Engineers through its Civil Works Program maintains most of our waterways. Maps of rivers and coastal waters are available from them. They will also send you information on lock regulations for the various canals. Boat and navigation regulations can differ from area to area. The U.S. Coast Guard is your source for this information.

The marinas are the commercial docking areas. Most of them provide waste-disposal areas and water and electrical connections. A boating enthusiast can live on the mooring for several days with the facilities they provide. Others are hotels with restaurants and swimming pools that have docking facilities so that you can take advantage of their luxury accommodations. Marina fees are much more expensive than those at autogrounds. ●

It may prove more feasible for you to rent rather than to buy a power boat. It will certainly pay for you to investigate the relative merits of each.

CHAPTER 11

THE FIRST CAMPER

■ Who was the first camper? This question was first posed to me by my eleven year old son. The question entered his mind as we were sitting around a campfire on one of our frequent weekend camping trips. That one question was the signal for the rest of the family to join in trying to unravel the answer. My fifteen year old son, who believes he is the smartest person in the world, (what teenager doesn't consider himself just that) suggested that it was the American Indian. This was immediately rejected by my thirteen year old daughter who felt that they might have been the masters of the outdoor life but they certainly were not the first. The baby interjected with some sound which we all ignored since we could not understand him.

There were several moments of silence while we all considered who might fill the description of the first camper. It was my wife who broke the silence by saying that the question was put wrong. We didn't understand what she meant until she explained herself. She felt that the question should not be who was the first camper but who were the first campers. The original question should have been plural and not singular. My wife, in her wisdom, had decided that the first campers were Adam and Eve. My eleven year old, who had posed the question in the first place, immediately rejected his mother's suggestion of Adam and Eve. His reasons seemed rather logical, although his mother never accepted them.

He felt that Adam and Eve did not have to concern themselves about shelter. They had no fear of the elements and survival was not a reality to them. Their only admonition was to avoid the forbidden fruit.

Once again silence fell on the members of my camping party only to be broken by Mitch, my eleven year old, who decided that he had the answer to his own question. He proudly announced that it was his conclusion, after much deep thought, that the first camper was the cave man.

Matt, my fifteen year old, felt that the caveman could not be considered the first camper because he did not provide his own shelter. He lived in a cave which he did not build himself and that cave was a permanent dwelling.

Mitch destroyed that argument very simply by explaining that when the caveman needed food he would have to leave his cave dwelling and roam far and wide until he found it. While the caveman was hunting this food he would sometimes get lost and not be able to get back to his cave. If it was raining, the caveman would have to find shelter or make his own. The shelter that might have kept him comfortable through the stormy night could have been made from leafy branches and therefore that made him the first camper.

I had to admit that the boy was thinking while everyone, except his mother who still held to her Adam and Eve theory, agreed that it was hard to argue against Mitchell's logic.

The conversation did not lag there. It was just the beginning. My daughter, Noelle, decided that at some point in the caveman's existence he must have realized that when he had to wander far away from his cave for food he would sometimes have to consume all of the game he had killed before he could get back to where he had started from. It was at this point that he must have left his cave along with his family whenever he went hunting. Until he killed his food, and after he killed his food, he would need shelter. That shelter would be the same type of animal skins that he was using for his clothing. He might have discovered how to join several of them together and then hold them up with saplings or tree branches. So the caveman was now attributed with having made the first tent.

We left the caveman and went on through history trying to think of all the people who had been campers. The Roman Legions in their pursuit to conquer the world, slept in tents. Then they spoke of the nomads who lived in tents and folded them up to wander until they found new grazing lands for their cattle. The American Indian was definitely talked of again. The way he was able to survive in the cold and the rain

and snow. Then the Pilgrims who had to live in tents before they could build their log cabins. The Conquistadores in South America. The American explorers Marquette and Joliet, Daniel Boone, Lewis and Clark. Trail blazers like Jim Bridger and Kit Carson. Camping for all of those people in the past was not done for fun. It was actually a way of life for them.

One of the best known present day campers is probably Sir Edmund Hillary. He camped out until he was able to reach the summit of Mount Everest. Thor Heyerdahl is probably the most outstanding boat camper because of his trip across the Pacific Ocean on the Raft, Kon-Tiki.

We sometimes tend to forget that there are people in this world who still do not live in houses or apartment buildings. In Northern Siberia there is a tribe that lives in a CHOOM. This is a bell shaped tent. KOTES, a tent made of reindeer skin is the home of the Laplanders of Northern Sweden. Seal-skin TUPEKS shelter the Eskimos of Labrador while TOLDOS made of Sea-Lion skin is the year round home of the Patagonians. Wandering Mongolian tribesmen live in felt covered YURTS. In Arabia and North Africa the Bedouin tribesmen are protected from the sun and the desert winds by BEITS or KHAIMAS. These tents are so large that they are often divided into several rooms.

All of this information was not put forth by just one person around our campfire. Everyone was animatedly involved and I am sure that the conversation would have carried itself into the realm of camping in outer-space when Mitchell, who posed the original question, suddenly expressed another thought. He wondered if any of us would enjoy camping so much if we had to live in a tent 365 days of the year?

The entire family was in agreement on this point. They loved camping. They looked forward to those special weekends and vacation time where we would camp out in the woods or on a beach. They liked setting up the tents and chopping firewood. There wasn't one chore associated with camping that they wanted to complain about or shirk. But whether or not they would enjoy it as much if it was a part of their daily lives they could not truthfully answer.

I felt that I could include this one instance out of the many happy ones that my family and I have had camping over the years. It seemed somehow to make a point about one of the ways a family can find harmony together. All of my children are enthusiastic campers. Even when we are not on a camping trip they are thinking ahead to some new area that we might explore or working on some new device that we can take along on our trip because it will come in handy.

We find no generation gap existing between our children and ourselves and we don't expect one. Sitting around a campfire has made it very easy for our children to bring up all kinds of subjects to talk about. They know that we are not unapproachable and the ease of conversation that takes place around the campfire transfers itself to our home so that we are in constant communication with our children.

I think that I can sum up what camping has meant to my family by telling you of an incident that did not occur on a camping trip.

We had finished dinner and my wife and I were sitting in the living room. The children came straggling in as they each finished their homework. The conversation covered many subjects and finally worked its way around to my fifteen year old who was talking about his future. He spoke about going to college and about not going to college. He expressed a desire to join the Air Force or the Marines. I'm sure that he spoke no differently than many other fifteen year old boys but what made this one time so unqiue was when he suddenly stopped in the middle of his monologue to ask me a question. I think the question is important enough to be quoted directly.

"Dad . . . When I grow up can I still go on camping trips with you and the family?"

KNOTS AND LASHING

All good camp crafters are familiar with the art of lashing. It can stand them in good stead whether they are on a one day hiking trip or an extended stay in the wilderness. A tripod to hold a water bag can be lashed together or an A-frame made from saplings to hold a tarpaulin. You can have a nice relaxing afternoon in a hammock if you know how to lash it between two trees. There are a hundred and one things that can be done around a camp when you know how to ·lash using string, cord, twine or rope. String, cord, and twine will be used on jobs that would be too clumsy for rope.

Before we tell you how to rig some lashings and tie some knots you should know a little something about rope.

MANILA HEMP:
For all around use this is the best rope.

NYLON:
Becoming increasingly popular. It is neat, light, strong and weatherproof. Drawbacks are that it is slippery making it hard to tie, it stretches, it is very expensive.

CLOTHESLINE:
No good. It stretches and it is very weak. It also swells when it is wet making it impossible to work and freezes solid when it is cold.

POLYETHYLENE ROPE:
Best rope for boating because it floats. Makes a better clothesline.

Nothing will last very long if it is not cared for and rope is no exception to that rule. It must be stored properly if it is to maintain its strength and usefulness. The ends should be whipped, tied with string or tape, to prevent abrasion and fraying. Hemp will mildew and rot if coiled and stored when wet. It must be left uncoiled and allowed to dry thoroughly. Open flame or intense heat will turn a nylon rope into a blob. Kinks and knots weaken a rope. They bend the fibers. That is why you should not tie any more knots than are necessary in any rope. All rope should be coiled carefully and stored in a dry place.

A rope that is whipped will not only look better but it will stay intact and will handle easier. The tape and string mentioned are for temporary whipping to prevent raveling when there is little time to do the proper job. If the rope is small enough you can also make an overhand knot at the end. To properly whip your rope you will need a piece of string about 12 inches long and proceed as the following directions indicate.

Take one end of the string and make a loop approximately two inches long. Lay the loop along the end of the rope. Both the short and the long end of the rope should hang over the end of the rope. With thumb and forefinger hold the loop of the string on the rope and begin winding the string down the length of the rope. You must start winding down the length of the rope. Part of the short end of the string should be extended from the end of the rope. Be sure that you wind neatly and tightly away from the end of the rope. Keep sliding your thumb back toward the end of the loop. You should only wrap enough string around the rope to cover 3/4 of an inch without covering up the loop. When you have finished winding, take the end of the string and slip it through the loop and pull it tight. Take the short end of the cord that is hanging over the end of the rope and begin to pull it. The loop with the other end of the cord through it will begin to pull up under the string that is around the rope and disappear. Keep pulling until you think the loop is about half way up the middle of the winding. Use a scissor to cut both ends of the cord. You can test the whipping by trying to push it off the rope. If it comes off of the rope the whipping is no good and you will have to start over again. If it remains on the rope you have done it right the first time.

And now to show you how to make some knots that are most commonly used around a camp.

B. Bend the end that is in your right hand over to the left. This will make a loop that will lay along the knot that is already made.

C. You will now see that the end you are holding in your left hand has only one place to go and that is into the loop.

D. Take the knot in both hands and pull the ends in opposite directions. This will tighten it. Pushing toward the center of the knot will loosen it. Left handed persons can tie this knot by reversing the process.

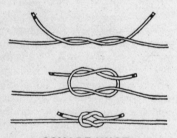

SQUARE KNOT:

The square knot is used for joining two ends of rope, cord or string of approximately the same size. This could be a shoestring or two ropes which you would like to make into one.

A. You have two pieces of rope . . . Pick up one end of each rope . . . one in each hand. Take the end in your right hand and cross it over the end in your left hand. Twist it back and down and then up in front. This gives you a single knot and your left hand is now holding the end that you started with.

SHEET BEND:

The square knot joins two pieces of rope of approximately the same thickness. The SHEET BEND will join two pieces of rope of different thicknesses. Actually the SHEET BEND is a square knot with a twist in it.

A. Take the two ropes of different thicknesses and make a square knot. Pull the ropes to tighten them. The smaller of the two will slip out.

B. To prevent the knot from slipping, cross the end of the smaller rope under the other piece of the same rope. Bring it up and over the loop of the thicker rope. At this point when you look at the knot you will see one end of the small rope onto and one end underneath the loop of the thicker rope. Pull the knot tight. The extra twist will prevent the smaller rope from slipping through and your knot will hold. The extra twist should be made with the smaller rope.

The name sheet bend was handed down to us by the early sailors. Ropes were not called ropes but "sheets" and "Bending" was the term used for making loops. Thus the term SHEET BEND.

BOWLINE:

There are times when you would like to have a loop in the end of a rope that will remain the same size that you made it, with no slipping. You might need it to slip over a peg or around a pole or a post. The knot you need is the BOWLINE.

A. Decide how big a loop you need and place your left hand where you want the knot. The

rope should lie across the palm of your left hand.

B. Use your right hand to make a loop that will come up and in back of the fingers of your left hand. As it comes down in the front clasp the rope with your left thumb where it crosses over.

C. Still holding the rope with the thumb and forefinger of your left hand, take the end of the rope with your right hand and pass it up from below and into the small loop.

D. Pull the end through the loop. It will make the main loop of the knot. Pass the end of the rope in back of the standing part of the rope. Then back to the front again and then down into the small loop again so that it rests beside itself.

E. The knot will pull up tight when you take the two pieces of rope in one hand and the main part of the rope in the other hand and pull in opposite directions.

The old sailing ship sailors were able to make this knot with one hand while holding onto the rigging with the other. If you can learn to make this knot with just one hand you are really good. Remember that this knot is made with just one end of the rope.

CLOVE HITCH:

This knot will not remain tight when one end is tied to an object that will move such as a boat or horse.

A. One end of the rope is held in

Bowline

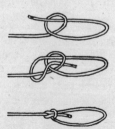

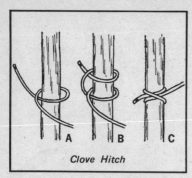

Clove Hitch

can practice these lashings using some twine or string. You will also need three sticks, each about 12 inches long. They should be as straight and smooth as possible and as thick as your thumb. The twine or string should be about three feet long. Try the square lashing first and practice it over and over again until you have it down pat.

SQUARE LASHING:

A. Hold your two sticks as pictured in the illustration. Use one end of the cord to tie a clove hitch to the verticle stick. Slip the knot around until the long length of the cord pulls out from the knot. Do not pull back against the knot but pull so that the knot tightens.

B. Bend the cord down around the horizontal stick then in back of the verticle stick so that the cord is back where it started. Repeat this procedure several times pulling the cord tightly as you go and placing the cord neatly as you go. Always follow the square and do not criss-cross the cord over the center, top or underneath the sticks.

C. If the sticks are holding firm, the binding can be tightened with a FRAPPING. Frapping is when the cord is wound between the two sticks pulling the first binding together tightly.

D. It is finished off with two half hitches around one stick. The end of the binding cord can be joined to the end of the starting cord with a square knot.

the right hand while the rest of the rope lies across the left palm going from right to left, pass the end of the rope around the back of a post. This should make an X at the front of the post and it should be held loosely away from the post between the left thumb and forefinger. The thumb should be on top and the fingers should be pointing to the right.

B. Bring the rope around the post for another turn from right to left but make it lower than the first turn with the end coming around under the X and between the two turns. The end will point to the right while the long piece of rope leads off to the left. Pull the end and the long piece of rope in opposite directions.

C. This knot can be untied quickly by doubling the short end. This gives you a loop which slips in under the X. Pull the loop to tighten, pull the end to untie.

Now that we have instructed you in a few knots we will show you how to rig some lashings. You

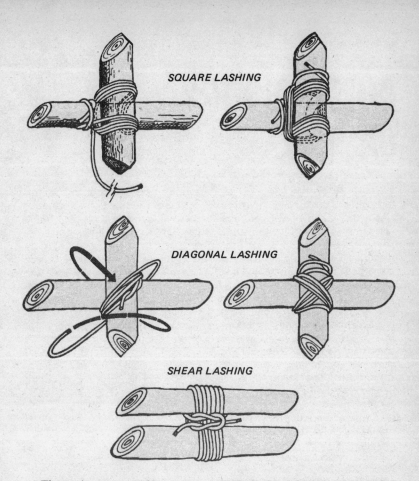

SQUARE LASHING

DIAGONAL LASHING

SHEAR LASHING

The ends can be stuffed underneath the lashing.

DIAGONAL LASHING:

A. Use two sticks to form an X as illustrated. They are held in this position continually.

B. A clove hitch is made around both sticks. Take three turns around one fork and three turns around the other fork. Pull tight.

C. Frap the end as you did in the square lashing.

SHEAR OR ROUND LASHING:

A. Take two sticks and place them as pictured in the illustration. Make a clove hitch around one stick. Take about five or six turns around each stick. The turns must lie neatly side by side.

B. It is finished off by frapping and ending with two half hitches or joining the ends using a square knot. Ends are stuffed under the lashing. ●

CHAPTER 12

COLD COUNTRY CAMPING

SNOWMOBILES

■ I can't think of any invention since the rumble seat that has given me as much pleasure as the snowmobile and there are half a million other people who must agree with me because that is how many snowmobiles have been sold up to now. I don't see how we ever got along without one. They are a definite necessity where we live in the mountains as we are somewhat isolated from civilization. We are 6 and a half miles from town (The town has three houses a general store and a filling station.) but most of that 6 and a half miles is coming down steep mountain hills. It only takes a couple of inches of snow, or even less, to make a car useless on those hills. With a snowmobile I never have to worry about getting down into town to do some food shopping when the roads are bad. In my house nobody ever argues about who is going to drive the car but who gets to drive the snowmobile.

Just like some campers who litter and pollute camping areas, there are snowmobilers causing trouble too. It seems that some of these people derive some sort of sadistic pleasure out of running elk, deer, coyotes and many other animals until the poor things drop dead from exhaustion. Because of these inhumane acts by these people, several states are contemplating severe restrictions on the use of snowmobiles. It is a pity that so many people will have to pay the penalty because of the criminal actions of so few.

Your choice of snowmobiles is pretty varied since there are close to fifty different manufacturers with as many different designs, power ratings, accessories and PRICES. The majority of these vehicles have single or twin-cylinder air-cooled engines. There are a few manufacturers putting them out with rotary engines. Almost all the transmissions are automatic, torque-sensitive with variable speed units. The horsepower is anywhere from 15 to 35. Snow conditions and terrain affect the speed but cruising along at 50 miles an hour is not unusual. The vehicle is driven by a cleated endless belt track, while bicycle or motorcycle type handle bars control the steering with one or a pair of short skis at the front of the machine. A good second hand machine can sell for two or three hundred dollars. A fancy new one can cost as much as $1,500 if not more.

The "buddy system" is a
snowmobile must.

Hills are a cinch for a good machine.

Vast territory can be covered easily.

You can learn to drive one of these machines in ten or fifteen minutes. After one hour you are practically an expert. This sport is not without its dangers. The conditions under which the snowmobile is sometimes operated can be very hazardous. One of the first safety rules for snowmobiles is never to go on a trip alone. Two is the rule for swimming but three is the rule for snowmobiles. It is after all only a machine and it can develop mechanical problems. If this should happen in several feet of snow such as light, deep powder or heavy wet corn snow you could have difficulty getting out on foot. Slush could be total disaster. Don't neglect to think about the natural hazards too. Breaking through the ice on a pond or lake, ploughing into a windfall and in the mountains falling into a crevasse. If any of these things did happen to you and you were not injured you would still have one heck of a time trying to recover your machine.

Snowmobiling is still safer than flying and a heck of a lot more fun. Snowmobile clubs are blossoming up all over the country. They arrange cross-country tours, races, rallies and even picnics.

Snowmobiles can take you into areas that are inaccessible to other recreational vehicles and so it has been a boon to winter camping. Naturally shelter is necessary when you go on a winter camping trip and someone came up with a sno-camper. This sno-camper is just like a tent trailer except that instead of being on wheels it is on runners. It contains a collapsible tent with plenty of storage space. I'm sure you know without my telling you that it is pulled behind the snowmobile.

Don't spoil your winter camping trip because of mechanical difficulties. Tune up the engine before you start out and take along a tool kit and some spare parts for your machine. A collapsible shovel is a must as is spare gas and oil. Your clothing is of prime importance. The heavily-insulated snowmobile suits that cover you from head to toe are excellent. Just make sure that you, get the best because when you are traveling along with nothing between you and the wind except your clothing you don't want to suddenly find out that it is not protecting you. There is a considerable chill factor that you must never forget about. If you travel 15 miles an hour on a calm day with a temperature of 20 degrees you will actually be traveling in a temperature of minus 5 degrees. Now you keep increasing your speed and the temperature keeps dropping. You can just imagine how cold it can

be if you are bucking a headwind. Standard protective clothing for this kind of weather is face mask, goggles, down insulated snowmobile suit, special boots and if you can get them to work, electric socks. You can develop a very bad case of frostbite riding this machine so don't take any chances. Snow blindness is also an ever-present danger which is easily prevented with the use of dark or slit goggles. They should be worn constantly while driving during the daylight hours.

If you are bogged down in the snow and you are going to have to walk out, be sure to carry as much food and water along with you as you can manage. Fire-starting materials are a must for you in the snow. If it is very cold and you want to rest or even sleep you can do so without the fear of freezing. Hollow out a cave in a snow drift. Line the bottom with pine boughs to keep you off the cold floor. Start a small fire in your snow cave, leaving an opening for ventilation. Snow is an excellent insulator and your fire will supply plenty of heat. •

Since the advent of the all-terrain vehicle, it is possible to travel anywhere on land, water, in swamp, sand or snow, safely, economically and in comfort.

CHAPTER 13

FIRST AID

FIRST AID

■ No matter how minor an injury or illness is, scratch or scrape or slight cold, it should receive treatment. Scratches or scrapes should be cleaned with an antiseptic or soap and water and minor sore throats and colds should be treated by gargling with salt water, keeping warm and resting.

GENERAL FIRST AID INFORMATION

A. The injured party should be kept lying down in a comfortable position. The head should be kept level with the body until you determine just how serious the injury is. If it is serious then the injured party should be maintained in that position until he can be safely moved.

B. When attempting to determine what injuries have taken place start with this order: 1. Serious bleeding: 2. stoppage of breathing: 3. poisoning: 4. shock: 5. wounds: 6. burns: 7. fractures: 8. dislocations: The immediate treatment of numbers 1, 2, and 3 is imperative and must be done at once before anything else.

C. The injured person must be kept warm.

D. While one person is trying to determine the extent of the injuries or giving first aid another person should be attempting to find a doctor or an ambulance.

E. Remain clam. Do not move the injured party or allow him to move himself unless you have no alternative.

F. No water or liquid of any kind is to be administered to an unconscious person.

IMMEDIATE ACTION

Delay in treating some injuries can be very serious. SHOCK: Seriously injured persons must receive treatment at once or they can develop shock. If you wait until the symptoms of shock develop then you will have twice as much trouble on your hands. The patient is in shock when you notice the following symptoms.

1. Pale face.
2. Shallow and irregular breathing.
3. Nausea.
4. Cool and moist skin.
5. Weak pulse.

TREATMENT FOR SHOCK

A. Cover the patient above and below to conserve body heat. External heat is never applied unless the weather is extremely cold. Do not make the patient hot, just comfortable.

B. The patient must be kept on his back with his feet raised.

C. Liquid nourishment is permissible unless the patient is

Do you know how to restore the breath of life?

1 Place one hand under victim's neck and lift. Tilt head back as far as possible by holding the crown of the head with your other hand.

2 Pull chin upward until the head is tilted back fully. This is essential for keeping the air passage open.

3 Place your mouth tightly over victim's mouth. Pinch nostrils shut. Breathe hard enough to make the chest rise. For babies and very young children, cover both nose and mouth tightly with your mouth. (For an adult, breathe vigorously about 12 times a minute. For a small child, take relatively short breaths, about 20 per minute.)

4 Remove mouth. Listen for sound of returning air. If you don't hear it, recheck head position. Breathe again. If you still get no air exchange, turn victim on side and slap between shoulders to dislodge foreign matter. Repeat breathing, removing mouth each time for escape of air. Don't give up. If possible, call a physician.

unconscious or has an abdominal injury. (WHEN THE HEAD OR CHEST HAVE SUSTAINED INJURY OR YOU NOTICE A FLUSH ON THE PATIENTS FACE AS THOUGH HE HAS SUNSTROKE THEN THE PATIENT MUST BE KEPT LYING DOWN WITH HIS HEAD HIGHER THAN HIS FEET).

TREATMENT OF WOUNDS WITH SEVERE BLEEDING

A. Place a thick layer of gauze on the wound and apply pressure until a bandage can be placed. Find the appropriate arterial pressure point and press it with your finger to stop the flow of blood.

B. If bleeding is from a limb a tourniquet may be applied. (**A TOURNIQUET SHOULD BE APPLIED ONLY IN CASES OF ARTERIAL BLEEDING AS IT CAN CAUSE SERIOUS INJURY**). Where arterial bleeding is indicated professional medical assistance is of immediate need. Once the tourniquet has been applied it should be released only by a doctor or some other qualified medical person. However, the tourniquet should be loosened at 15 minute intervals to prevent gangrene.

C. Treatment for shock should be given immediately upon staunching the flow of blood.

SMOKE INHALATION, ASPHYXIATION, STOPPAGE OF BREATHING

A. Begin artificial respiration at once.

B. Patient should be moved into the open or clear air.

C. Clothing should be loosened.

D. Remove any obstructions to breathing in the patients mouth.

E. Check for wounds.

F. Begin treatment for shock.

ARTIFICIAL RESPIRATION

Nothing should delay the immediate application of artificial respiration to any person who has suffered smoke inhalation, asphyxiation or stoppage of breathing. Moving the patient to an ideal location or waiting for mechanical equipment is a waste of valuable time. Do not use the old prone pressure method or the back pressure-arm lift method or the back pressure hip-lift method. These techniques are outmoded and prove to be inadequate when compared to mouth to mouth or mask to mouth resuscitation. If you are in the wilderness it is doubtful that you will have the mechanical equipment to apply the mask-to-mouth method, so we will concentrate on mouth-to-mouth resuscitation. The victim must be placed on his back. Do not be concerned about contracting any infection or disease. The possibility is very remote. Make sure that the air passageway is not obstructed. Air will not enter the patients lungs if the air passage is obstructed. The three main causes for obstructions in the air passage are ... 1. Liquid, false teeth, or foreign matter in the mouth and throat. 2. Relaxation of the jaw causes the tongue to fall back and block the throat. 3. When the head is bent forward with the chin close to the chest it "kinks" the throat and blocks the air passage. To unkink the throat, you place your hand under the back of the victim's neck and lift up gently. The head should tilt back slightly so that his nose is pointing up and at a slight backward angle. Pull his lower jaw forward.

STEPS FOR PERFORMING ARTIFICIAL OR MOUTH-TO-MOUTH RESPIRATION

A. Place the victim on his back.

B. Clear the victim's nose, mouth and throat. If these are clear begin mouth-to-mouth exhaled air method at once. If vomit or mucus can be seen in the mouth, nose and throat, clean it away quickly with a cloth, or with a sweeping motion pass the index and middle fingers through the victim's throat.

C. Tilt the patient's head back so that his nose is pointing up and slightly backwards. Remember the throat must be unkinked so you can pull his head back until his neck looks stretched.

D. Kneel at the victim's left side. Place your thumb in the middle of the patient's mouth hooking your thumb behind his lower teeth and pull his lower jaw forcefully outward. His lower teeth should be occluded behind his upper teeth. The jaw should be held in this position as long as the victim remains unconscious. Protect your thumb from injury from the victim's teeth by wrapping a cloth around it.

E. Compress the victim's nose between the thumb and forefinger of your right hand.

F. Inhale deeply and cover the victim's open mouth with your open mouth. Make sure there is airtight contact. Exhale rapidly until his chest rises. Forceful exhalation into adults. Gentle exhalation into children.

G. As soon as you see the victim's chest rise you immediately break lip contact with him and let him exhale without any help from you. If the victim's chest does not rise when you exhale into his mouth you must improve the support of his air passage and exhale more forcefully. These lung inflations should occur 12 to 20 times per minute. Do not stop until the victim begins to breathe or he is pronounced dead by a qualified authority.

All injuries do not require the immediate action as those we have just described but all injuries should be treated without too much delay.

BURNS:

The chief dangers resulting from burns are shock and infection. Your main concern should be to relieve pain, prevent infection and administer treatment for shock.

MINOR BURNS:

Require the application of sterile petroleum or burn ointment. The pain can be alleviated with snow or ice packs.

SEVERE BURNS:

Severe burns usually bring on shock. Loose clothing should be cut or torn away from the burned area. If clothing is fused to the burned area do not attempt to remove it. Only qualified medical persons should attempt to remove the clothing that is stuck to a burn. If the clothing can be removed, use the same medication as described for minor burns and then apply a snug bandage. Olive oil can be substituted for the above mentioned medication. Do not use commercially prepared salad oils as they may contain vinegar. Another medication that can be prepared by you is a solution containing three tablespoons of baking soda or Epsom salts mixed in one quart of warm water. Soak a bandage or clean cloths and apply to the burned area. The patient should be kept covered and warm.

BROKEN OR DISLOCATED BONES

If you are unable to determine whether the bone is broken or dislocated then treat it as a broken bone.

A. It is essential that the patient not be moved until the fracture has been immobolized by a splint. Only extreme circumstances should make you disregard this cardinal rule.

B. Boards, wire, blankets, pillows, folded coats and tree limbs can be used as substitutes for immobilizing materials. Wire, boards and tree limbs should be padded for comfort.

C. The joints above and below the break should be immobilized. This necessitates the making of an extra long splint.

MINOR BLEEDING WOUNDS

A. Clean the wound with a mild antiseptic or plain soap and water.

B. The wound should be covered with a sterile bandage or dressing.

SPRAINS

A. Elevate the sprained limb

B. Use cold applications on the affected part. Cold cloths, Ice packs.

C. Severe sprains should have proper medical attention.

EXPOSURE TO COLD

Persons exposed to excessively low temperatures over extended periods of time tend to become numb and therefore find movement difficult. An irresistible drowsiness envelops them. Their eyesight fails, they stagger and fall and they may lose consciousness.

If a stoppage of breathing has occured, artificial respiration should be started immediately. If it is at all possible the victim should be taken inside a shelter. Wrap him in blankets or a sleeping bag as you must try to warm him as quickly as possible. If water is available along with a tub (very unlikely in the wilderness) the water should be warm, NOT HOT. The temperature of the water should be between 78 and 82 degrees F. If he begins to react induce him to drink hot liquids. As soon as he is revived enough to terminate the water treatment, dry him thoroughly and get him to where he can receive professional medical attention.

UPSET STOMACH

Severe vomiting usually accompanies an upset stomach. Proper medical attention should be sought immediately as attacks of vomiting can be controlled with ginger ale, Coca-Cola or Coca-Cola syrup. Kaopectate would help to relieve any diarrhea that might be involved.

INFECTIONS AND FEVERS

If a patient's temperature cannot be lowered to normal by using aspirin and sponging his body and forehead with damp cloths he should be taken to where he can receive professional medical attention without delay. Infections may require antibiotics and these should be administered only by a doctor.

FLU

Until you can get the patient to a doctor keep him warm and comfortable. Give him two aspirin tablets every four hours and have him drink large amounts of water and fruit juices.

HEADACHE

Two aspirin tablets every four hours. If this does not help try an ice pack on the head or in back of the neck. The ice pack can be made with snow if there is any available.

ABDOMINAL INJURY, SEVERE

If the injury to the abdomen is so severe that the intestines are protruding, DO NOT ATTEMPT TO FORCE THEM BACK IN! Keep the victim lying on his back and cover the wound with a sterile salt pack. Water can be sterilized by boiling it for 15 or 20 minutes. The salt can be in the water when it is being boiled. Since the bandage must be sterile too, drop it into the water and let it boil for the same length of time as the water. If you are in an isolated area and you cannot get medical attention or make communication so that a helicopter can come in to remove the patient, you will have to carry him out on a stretcher. An abdominal wound such as described here can occur when someone falls and the abdomen is penetrated by a sharp rock or piece of dead tree.

EATING WILD GAME

All wild game, no matter how small or how large, should be well cooked before eating. All wild game should be considered carriers of trichinosis and this is passed on to human beings through the eating process. There is no danger if you overcook it.

Tularemia, also known as "deer fly fever" and "rabbit fever" is a highly contagious disease that can be contracted merely by handling infected rodents, squirrels, hares, etc. In cases of extreme emergency the flesh of an infected animal can be eaten. BUT IT MUST BE OVERCOOKED!

Any person bitten by any animal in a wilderness area must not delay in seeking medical attention. Rabies is still an ever-present danger. A broader description of the action to take when bitten was described in an earlier chapter.

HEAT CAN BE A TREATMENT

Stomach cramps and muscular pains can be eased with heat. Towels or clean rags can be cooked in a pot of water over an open campfire. When the desired temperature is attained, the towels are removed from the pot of hot water, wrung out and folded neatly and applied to the aching stomach or muscle. Rocks placed very close to a campfire will retain heat and when they are wrapped in cloths or towels they can be placed at a patients feet or along the side of his body to keep him warm. Be careful and don't burn the patient. DO NOT USE

HEAT IF THERE IS ANY SUSPICION OF APPENDICITIS. For a case of suspected appendicitis it is best to use cold packs applied to the right side of the abdomen. Reduction of infected and swollen limbs due to the infection can be attained by soaking the affected limb in hot water. Infections on the body are treated with hot packs. The best method is a half hour immersion every two hours.

VINEGAR AS MEDICATION

Vinegar is an excellent treatment for insect stings and bites.

BICARBONATE OF SODA

The old standby for the harried business man with a sour or acid stomach. Add a teaspoonful to a glass of warm water and drink.

The pain of insect stings and bites can be relieved by applying wet packs made with bicarbonate of soda. The pain of minor burns can be reduced with wet soda packs as well as the itch that accompanies poison oak, poision ivy and poison sumac.

MEDICAL SUPPLIES

The following list is only a suggestion as to what medical supplies should be in your medicine chest when you are going on an extended camping trip into a wilderness area. In some states it may be necessary to obtain a doctor's prescription in order to purchase several of the suggested medicines. We suggest that you visit your family doctor to show him this list. Tell him about your plans for the camping trip. He may agree with everything that is on this list or he may not agree and substitute some other medication. In all instances we suggest that you follow your doctor's advice. His knowledge in these matters is superior to yours and mine.

6—½ grain Codeine sulphate tablets. Used only for pain.

100—Aspirin, Anacin or Bufferin tablets. 5 grain. Used for joint pains, headaches and reduction of fever.

12—Gantrimycin (Roche) tablets. Your doctor will recommend the size. Used as substitute for penicillin. Dosage as recommended by your doctor for treatment of infection or pneumonia.

1—2 oz. tube of zinc oxide ointment. Used to protect nose and face from sunburn.

7—5 oz. squeeze bottles of Phisohex or bars of white soap. Used for cleaning hands and wounds.

1—Large bottle of Kaopectate. Used for diarrhea. Follow directions on the bottle.

1—1 oz. bottle of Tr. Merthiolate, 1-1000. Used for wound disinfectant.

1—¼ oz. butyn eye ointment. Used for treatment of eye inflammations and snow blindness. Your doctor will prescribe treatment.

1—1 oz. tube cod liver oil-Vaseline ointment, 50-50. Used for burns.

1—2 oz. bottle of elixir of terpin hydrate with codeine. Used for coughs. In some states this can only be purchased by prescription. Your doctor will give you directions how to use this or he will substitute a patent medicine.

100—Halazone tablets. Used for purifying water.

1—Bottle of earache medicine. This should be suggested by your doctor.

1—½ oz. bottle of oil of cloves. Used to treat toothaches.

1—Large box of Q tips. Used as swabs for disinfecting wounds.

1—16 unit first aid kit. Add your favorite laxative. Include high potency Vitamins B complex and C. They will replace body needs weakened through accident or illness.

1—Unbreakable oral thermometer.

1—Ice-pack bag. Rubberized. Used to reduce swelling and for headaches.

1—Hot water bag. Rubberized. Used to treat shock or to keep your feet warm.

1—Snake bite kit. Suction type.

4—Malleable wire splints.

24—Safety pins. Mixed sizes.

1—Spool of silk ligature thread.

1—Bandage scissors. •

LIGHTNING

I don't know anyone who is not afraid of lightning. I am not afraid to admit that I am also afraid of lightning. I am fascinated by it but afraid of it because I know that it is dangerous. When I am out hiking and I see dark clouds beginning to gather I don't wait to hear the thunder or see the lightning, I head right for shelter as fast as I can.

There are some places that are more dangerous than others during a lightning storm and it is best that you avoid them. The top of a hill or a mountain is no place to be when the sky is so fully charged with electricity. Standing under a number of trees that are shorter and a little distance away from tall trees is considered safer.

If you are on open ground during a shower and there is thunder and lightning in the sky, don't try to run to shelter if it is too far away. Lie down in the field. It is a much better feeling to be wet than to be struck by a bolt of lightning.

You can lightning-proof your camp site by stringing #6 wire between the trees over the campsite. This same wire must be long enough so that it will hang down both tree trunks to the ground and then stretch 10 or twelve feet along the trail heading away from the campsite.

If you are swimming, get out of the water and into shelter. If you are in a boat, wood, fiberglass or metal, it does not matter, get to shore and shelter at once. If you are on the beach get to a safe place. In all instances you should not wait to do these things when the lightning and thunder are overhead. Get to shelter well in advance of the arrival of the storm. •

CHAPTER 14

NATIONAL PARK INFORMATION & DIRECTORY

ACADIA:

Superintendent, Big Bend National Park, Big Bend National Park, Texas.

AREA: 1,106 square miles. Open all year.

LOCATION: Southwest Texas.

HIGHWAYS: U.S. 90, 385, Texas 118.

FACILITIES: 156 camp and picnic sites, cabins and meal service. Limited supplies.

TOWNS IN VICINITY: Alpine, Marfa and Sanderson.

ATTRACTIONS: Mountains and desert in the Great Bend of the Rio Grande. South boundary is border between U.S. and Mexico. Flora and fauna typical of Mexico.

BRYCE CANYON:

Superintendent, Bryce Canyon National Park, Bryce Canyon, Utah.

AREA: 56 square miles. Open all year.

LOCATION: Southern Utah.

HIGHWAYS: U.S. 89, Utah 12.

FACILITIES: Lodge opens from mid-June to mid-October. Camp and picnic sites.

TOWNS IN VICINITY: Mt. Carmel, Junction and Panguitch.

ATTRACTIONS: Box canyon where rain, snow and frost have carved colored pinnacles and spires.

CARLSBAD CAVERNS:

Superintendent, Carlsbad Caverns National Park, Box 111, Carlsbad, New Mexico.

AREA: 77 square miles. Open all year.

LOCATION: Southeast New Mexico.

HIGHWAYS: U.S. 62, 180, 285, New Mexico 54.

FACILITIES: Lunch room in caverns.

TOWNS IN VICINITY: Carlsbad, White City and Artesia.

ATTRACTIONS: Largest underground caverns ever discovered.

CRATER LAKE:

Superintendent, Crater Lake National Park, Box 672, Medford 4, Oregon.

AREA: 250 square miles. Open all year.

LOCATION: Southwest Oregon on the Crest of the Cascade Range.

HIGHWAYS: U.S. 97, 99. Oregon 62, 230.

FACILITIES: Hotel, cabins, and meals, picnic sites. 180 campsites. Fishing license not required.

ATTRACTIONS: Crater Lake which is the deepest lake on the North American continent. 1,983 feet deep.

EVERGLADES:

Superintendent, Everglades National Park, Box 275, Homestead, Florida.

AREA: 2,341 square miles. Open all year.

LOCATION: Southwest Florida.

HIGHWAYS: U.S. 1, 41, Florida 27.

FACILITIES: 115 campsites, picnic sites.

TOWNS IN VICINITY: Homestead and Florida City.

ATTRACTIONS: Largest subtropical wilderness in the U.S. Extensive fresh and salt water areas, mangrove forests, grassy prairies. Abundant wildlife.

GLACIER:

Superintendent, Glacier National Park, West Glacier, Montana.

AREA: 1,583 square miles. Open all year. Road conditions unpredictable after mid-September.

LOCATION: Rocky Mountains of Northwest Montana.

HIGHWAYS: U.S. 2, 89, 93, Montana 17, 49.

FACILITIES: Hotels, cabins, 255 campsites.

TOWNS IN VICINITY: Babb, Whitefish, West Glacier, East Glacier.

ATTRACTIONS: Beautiful mountain scenery, over 60 glaciers, more than 200 lakes, abundant wildlife ...

elk, deer, bighorn sheep, mountain goat, black and grizzly bear.

GRAND CANYON:
Superintendent, Grand Canyon National Park, Grand Canyon, Arizona.
AREA: 1,009 square miles. Open all year.
LOCATION: Northern Arizona.
HIGHWAYS: U.S. 66, 89, Arizona 64, 67.
FACILITIES: Meals, lodgings, 418 campsites.
TOWNS IN VICINITY: Fredonia, Cameron, Silliams, Flagstaff.
ATTRACTIONS: The world's most impressive spectacle. A chasm a mile deep and four to eighteen miles wide. A great multi-colored canyon carved millions of years ago by the Colorado River.

GRAND TETON:
Superintendent, Grand Teton National Park, Moose, Wyoming.
AREA: 484 square miles. Open mid-May to late October.
LOCATION: Covers the scenic portion of the Wyoming Teton Range as well as the northern portion of Jackson Hole, a high mountain valley.
HIGHWAYS: U.S. 89, 287, 26, 187, Wyoming 22.
FACILITIES: 545 campsites, cabins, lodges, Dude Ranches located outside of park.
TOWNS IN VICINITY: Driggs, Jackson, Alpine, Rexburg.
ATTRACTIONS: 7 large lakes, glaciers, snow fields, extensive evergreen forests. Mountain peaks, deep canyons. Tetons rise to 13,766 feet.

GREAT SMOKEY MOUNTAINS:
Superintendent, Great Smokey Mountains National Park, Gatlinburg, Tennessee.
AREA: 781 square miles. Open all year.
LOCATION: Tennessee and North Carolina.
HIGHWAYS: U.S. 442, 129, 64; Tennessee 68, 30, 71, 72, 73, 75.
FACILITIES: 538 campsites on the Tennessee side. 282 campsites on the North Carolina side. Lodgings and meals obtainable outside the park.
TOWNS IN VICINITY: In Tennessee: Gatlinburg, Parkerville, Benton, Madisonville, Maryville, Townsand, Pigeon, Forage, Cosby. North Carolina Side: Smokemont, Cherokee, Topton, Murphy, Duck Town, Isabella.
ATTRACTIONS: 200,000 acres of virgin forests. Great Smokey Mountains, 1,200 species of plants and shrubs.

HALEAKALA:
Superintendent, Haleakala National Park, Maui, Hawaii.
AREA: 26 square miles. Open all year. Can be reached by plane and boat daily from mainland. Scheduled flights leave daily from Honolulu to Kahului, Maui.
TOWNS IN VICINITY: Kahului and Hana.

ATTRACTIONS: 30 miles of riding and hiking trails. Silver sword plants and awesome Haleakala Crater. It is 7½ miles long, 2½ miles wide, 21 mile perimeter, and 3,000 feet deep. May 15 to Sept. 15, meals are available at Silver Sword Inn as well as lodgings.

HAWAII:
Superintendent, Hawaii Volcanoes National Park, Hawaii, Hawaii.

AREA: 266 square miles. Open all year.

FACILITIES: Meals and lodgings available in nearby towns.

TOWNS IN VICINITY: Hilo, Kamuela, Hawi, and Kailua.

ATTRACTIONS: Hiking trails, lookout points, exotic plants, birdlife. Its main attraction, the active volcanoes.

HOT SPRINGS:
Superintendent, Hot Springs National Park, Box 859, Hot Springs National Park, Arkansas.

AREA: 1.6 square miles. Open all year.

LOCATION: Central Arkansas in the Ouachita Mountains.

HIGHWAYS: U.S. 70, 270, Arkansas 7, 5.

FACILITIES: 25,000 people can be accommodated at the nearby hotels and lodging houses.

TOWNS IN VICINITY: Hot Springs, Mountain Valley and Mountain Pine.

ATTRACTIONS: 47 hot springs.

ISLE ROYALE:
Superintendent, Isle Royale National Park, 87 N. Ripley St., Houghton, Michigan.

AREA: 209 square miles. Open May 15 to November 1.

LOCATION: Upper Lake Superior near the International Boundary of Canada and the United States.

HIGHWAYS: No roads. Can be reached by plane and boat only.

FACILITIES: Wilderness area. Campgrounds are located at 6 points on the shores of the main island. Boats to island leave from Houghton and Copper Harbor, Michigan.

TOWNS IN VICINITY: Grand Marais and Frand Portage, Minnesota.

ATTRACTIONS: A 47 mile-long island that is from 5 to 9 miles wide. Very remote wilderness area with foot trails and largest Moose herd in North America.

KINGS CANYON:
Superintendent, Kings Canyon National Park, Three Rivers, California.

AREA: 710 square miles. Open all year.

LOCATION: The heart of the Sierra Nevada Range in East Central California.

HIGHWAYS: U.S. 99, California 65, 180, 198.

FACILITIES: Lodgings in the park and on private land at Wilsonia and Big Stump.

TOWNS IN VICINITY: Pinehurst, Miramonte, Badger, Fresno, Visalia.

ATTRACTIONS: The General Grant tree, which is the second largest living tree. Hundreds of miles of wilderness trails. Trails leading to peaks over 13,000 feet high.

LASSEN VOLCANIC:

Superintendent, Lassen Volcanic National Park, Mineral, California.

AREA: 165 square miles. Roads may be impassable from November through June.

LOCATION: Northeastern California at the southern end of the Cascade Range.

HIGHWAYS: U.S. 99, 299, 395. California 44, 89, 36.

FACILITIES: 456 campsites. Lodgings available at Manzanita Lake Lodge and at Drakesbad. Limited services at Juniper Lake.

TOWNS IN VICINITY: Chester, Mineral and Redding.

ATTRACTIONS: Dome-type volcanic peaks, Mt. Lassen is 10,453 feet above sea level. Practice caution in thermal areas. Steam and water are dangerous.

MAMMOTH CAVE:

Superintendent, Mammoth Cave National Park, Mammoth Cave, Kentucky.

AREA: 80 square miles. Open all year.

LOCATION: Southcentral Kentucky.

HIGHWAYS: U.S. 31W, 62, 68. Kentucky 62, 65.

FACILITIES: 37 Campsites. Lodgings and meals available in park.

TOWNS IN VICINITY: Glasgow, Cave City, Bowling Green, Mammoth Cave.

ATTRACTIONS: Caverns discovered in 1799.

MESA VERDE:

Superintendent, Mesa Verde National Park, Mesa Verde National Park, Colorado.

AREA: 80 square miles. Open all year.

HIGHWAYS: U.S. 160, 666, 550. Colorado 789.

FACILITIES: Summer only. Semi-permanent tent cottages with cots and bedding, lights and some furniture. 170 campsites.

TOWNS IN VICINITY: In Colorado, Durange, Silverton, Cortex. In New Mexico, Aztec, Shiprock.

ATTRACTIONS: 1,000 year old archeological preserve of Indian cliff-dwelling ruins.

MOUNT McKINLEY:

Superintendent, Mount McKinley National Park, McKinley Park, Alaska.

AREA: 3,030 square miles. Open June to September 15.

HIGHWAYS: Park road network connects with Denali Highway, Alaska 8. All roads closed in winter. 3,000 foot airport located near McKinley Park Hotel.

TOWNS IN VICINITY: Fairbanks, Paxson, Richardson, Windy, Carlo, Healy Fork, Garner.

ATTRACTIONS: Vast mountain wilderness with highest mountains in North Ameri-

ca. Glaciers, unusual wildlife.

MOUNT RAINIER:
Superintendent, Mount Rainier
National Park, Longmire,
Washington.
AREA: 377 square miles. Open
all year.
LOCATION: Southwestern
Washington in Cascade
Range.
HIGHWAYS: U.S. 410, 99,
Washington 5. Road to Para-
dise Valley open all year.
Other roads sometimes
blocked because of weather
in winter.
FACILITIES: 262 Campsites,
picnic sites. No overnight
accommodations in winter.
TOWNS IN VICINITY: Park-
way, Packwood, Longmire,
American River, Ashfork.
ATTRACTIONS: Mount
Rainier, 26 active glaciers,
beautiful Alpine scenery.

OLYMPIC:
Superintendent, Olympic National Park, 600 East Park
Ave., Port Angeles, Washington.
AREA: 1,406 square miles.
Open all year.
LOCATION: Olympic Penin-
sula in northwestern Washington.
HIGHWAYS: U.S. 101.
FACILITIES: 503 campsites,
picnic sites.
TOWNS IN VICINITY:
Sequim, Quinualt, Clear-
water, Amanda Park, Hood-
sport, Joyce Forks, La Push,
Port Angeles, Sappho.
ATTRACTIONS: Rushing
streams, rugged mountain
wilderness, glacier-clad
peaks, rain forests, wild
coastal strip, Mount Olym-
pus and famous Roosevelt
Elk.

PETRIFIED FOREST:
Superintendent, Petrified For-
est National Park, Holbrook,
Arizona.
AREA: 146 square miles. Open
all year.
LOCATION: Northeastern Ari-
zona.
HIGHWAYS: U.S. 66, 260,
Arizona 63.
FACILITIES: No camping al-
lowed. No overnight accom-
modations.
TOWNS IN VICINITY: Joseph
City, Holbrook, Navajo,
Chambers, Sanders, Concho.
ATTRACTIONS: 6 Petrified
Forests. Logs of agate and
jasper lying on the ground.
Ruins of prehistoric Indian
homes made of petrified
wood. Desert animals.

PLATT:
Superintendent, Platt National
Park, Box 379, Sulphur, Okla-
homa.
AREA: 146 square miles. Open
all year.
LOCATION: Southern Okla-
homa.
HIGHWAYS: U.S. 77, Okla-
homa 7, 18.
FACILITIES: Overnight ac-
commodations available in
towns.
TOWNS IN VICINITY: Gene
Autry, Chickasaw, Davis,
Springer, Sulphur.
ATTRACTIONS: Cold mineral
springs.

ROCKY MOUNTAIN:

Superintendent, Rocky Mountain National Park, Box 1086, Estes Park, Colorado.

AREA: 405 square miles. Open all year.

LOCATION: North-central Colorado at front range of Rocky Mountains.

HIGHWAYS: U.S. 34, Colorado 7, 16, 262, 278. Trans-mountain travel closed by weather from late May to mid-September.

FACILITIES: Meals and lodgings in park during summer only. Dude ranches, motels and lodges outside of park.

TOWNS IN VICINITY: Granby, Glen Haven, Estes Park, Allenspark, Gould, Grand Lake.

ATTRACTIONS: Snowcapped mountains, multi-colored canyons, Alpine lakes and streams, abundant wildlife.

SEQUOIA:

Superintendent, Sequoia National Park, Three Rivers, California.

AREA: 604 square miles. Open all year.

LOCATION: Eastern central California across the heart of the Sierra Nevadas.

HIGHWAYS: U.S. 99, California 65, 198, 180 and Generals Highway.

FACILITIES: 727 campsites, picnic grounds.

TOWNS IN VICINITY: Visalia, Fresno, Badger, Three Rivers, Wood Lake, Pinehurst.

ATTRACTIONS: General Sherman tree supposedly the largest living thing in the world and other groves of giant sequoias. Mount Whitney, gorges, canyons, rushing streams, Alpine lakes.

SHENANDOAH:

Superintendent, Shenandoah National Park, Luray, Virginia.

AREA: 302 square miles. Open all year.

LOCATION: The Blue Ridge Mountains of Virginia.

HIGHWAYS: U.S. 211, 522, 340, 33, Virginia 231, 276.

FACILITIES: Campsites for trailer and tent campers.

ATTRACTIONS: 105 miles of skyline drive through the park. Mountain and valley scenery.

NATIONAL FORESTS

Information on national forests can be obtained from: National Forest Headquarters, Forest Service, U.S. Department of Agriculture, Washington 25, D.C.

For information regarding regional national forests, address the regional supervisors at the following locations:

REGION 1
NORTHERN REGION

Headquarters, Federal Building, Missoula, Montana

FORESTS IN IDAHO

Clearwater National Forest, Orofino, Idaho.

Camp and picnic sites. Motels, cabins, and pack trip outfitters available.

Coeur d'Alene National Forest, Coeur d'Alene, Idaho

Seven camp sites, two picnic sites only.

Kaniksu National Forest,
Sandpoint, Idaho
> Twelve camp and picnic sites, three swimming sites, one winter sports area.

Nezperce National Forest,
Grangeville, Idaho
> Six campsites and one picnic site, hiking and horse trails wilderness pack trips, scenic drives.

St. Joe National Forest,
St. Maries, Idaho
> Eight camp and picnic sites, one swimming site, winter sports.

NATIONAL FORESTS
IN MONTANA

Beaverhead National Forest,
Dillon, Montana
> Twenty-eight camp and picnic sites, winter sports.

Bitterroot National Forest,
Hamilton, Montana
> Eleven camp and picnic sites, winter sports.

Custer National Forest,
Billings, Montana
> Thirteen camp sites, two picnic sites.

Deerlodge National Forest,
Butte, Montana
> Twenty-one camp sites, five picnic sites. Riding trails, wilderness trips.

Flathead National Forest,
Kalispell, Montana
> Fifteen campsites, one picnic site, two swimming sites. Winter sports.

Gallatin National Forest,
Bozeman, Montana
> Thirty-three camp and picnic sites. Primitive areas. Scenic drives, trail riding and wilderness trips. Winter sports.

Helena National Forest,
Helena, Montana
> Six campsites, two picnic sites. Hiking, boat trips. Horse trails and wilderness trips.

Kootenai National Forest,
Libby, Montana
> Five camp and picnic sites. Winter sports. Trail riding.

Lewis and Clark National Forest,
Great Falls, Montana
> Twelve camp and picnic sites. Wilderness trips, riding trails, scenic drives.

Lolo National Forest,
Missoula, Montana
> Eighteen camp sites, one picnic site, one swimming site. Wilderness pack trips, foot trails, scenic drives.

NATIONAL FORESTS
IN WASHINGTON

Colville National Forest,
Colville, Washington
> Sixteen camp and picnic sites, two swimming sites, scenic drives, winter sports.

REGION 2
ROCKY MOUNTAIN REGION
Headquarters, Federal Center, Building 85, Denver 7, Colorado

NATIONAL FORESTS
IN COLORADO

Arapaho National Forest,
Golden, Colorado
> Thirty-three camp sites, twenty

picnic sites, winter sports, riding trails, wilderness trips.

Grand Mesa-Uncompahgre National Forest, Delta, Colorado

Thirty-one camp sites, six picnic sites, winter sports, scenic drives, saddle trips.

Gunnison National Forest, Gunnison, Colorado

Thirty-four camp and picnic sites, winter sports, saddle trips, wilderness trips.

Pike National Forest, Colorado Springs, Colorado

Thirty-seven camp sites, forty picnic sites, scenic drives, winter sports.

Rio Grande National Forest, Monte Vista, Colorado

Thirty-one camp sites, five picnic sites, winter sports, saddle and pack trips, scenic drives.

Roosevelt National Forest, Fort Collins, Colorado

Twenty-one camp sites, 18 picnic sites, saddle and pack trips, scenic drives.

Routt National Forest, Steamboat Springs, Colorado

Forty-eight camp sites, five picnic sites, saddle and pack trips, scenic drives.

San Isabel National Forest, Pueblo, Colorado

Twenty-six camp and picnic sites, winter sports, scenic drives, saddle and pack outfits.

San Juan National Forest, Durango, Colorado

Thirty-four camp sites, seven picnic sites, scenic drives, winter sports, saddle and pack trips.

White River National Forest, Glenwood Springs, Colorado

Primitive area, fifty-eight camp sites, one picnic site, one swimming site, saddle and pack trails.

NATIONAL FORESTS IN NEBRASKA

Nebraska National Forest, Lincoln, Nebraska

Three camp sites, two picnic sites, one swimming site.

NATIONAL FORESTS IN SOUTH DAKOTA

Black Hills National Forest, Custer, South Dakota

Twenty-one camp sites, forty-five picnic sites, two swimming sites, winter sports.

NATIONAL FORESTS IN WYOMING

Bighorn National Forest, Sheridan, Wyoming

Primitive area, sixty camp sites, fourteen picnic sites, saddle and pack trips, scenic drives.

Medicine Bow National Forest, Laramie, Wyoming

Twenty-three camp sites, twenty-five picnic sites, winter sports, saddle and pack trips, scenic drives.

Shoshone National Forest, Cody, Wyoming

Thirty-four camp sites, two picnic sites, winter sports, saddle and pack trips, primitive area.

REGION 3 SOUTHWESTERN REGION

Headquarters, 510 2nd St., N.W., Alburquerque, New Mexico

NATIONAL FORESTS
IN ARIZONA

Apache National Forest,
Springerville, Arizona
Primitive area, twenty-six camp sites, one picnic site, boating (no motors), horse back riding, pack trips, hiking.

Coconino National Forest,
Flagstaff, Arizona
Eighteen camp sites, five picnic sites, boating, winter sports scenic drives.

Coronado National Forest,
Tucson, Arizona
Thirty-two camp sites, seventeen picnic sites, winter sports, swimming, scenic drives, pack trips, hiking trails.

Kaibab National Forest,
Williams, Arizona
Six camp and picnic sites.

Prescott National Forest,
Prescott, Arizona
Eight camp sites, eight picnic sites, horse trails, scenic drives.

Sitgreaves National Forest,
Holbrook, Arizona
Four camp and picnic sites, swimming, saddle and pack trips.

Tonto National Forest,
Phoenix, Arizona
Sixteen camp sites, twelve picnic sites, boating, swimming, saddle and pack trips, scenic drives.

NATIONAL FORESTS
IN NEW MEXICO

Carson National Forest,
Taos, New Mexico
Wilderness area.

Cibola National Forest,
Albuquerque, New Mexico
Fifteen camp sites, fifteen picnic sites, scenic drives, winter sports.

Gila National Forest,
Silver City, New Mexico
Twelve camp sites, three picnic sites, pack trips, primitive area, riding and hiking trails.

Lincoln National Forest,
Alamogorda, New Mexico
Ten camp sites, two picnic sites, winter sports, hiking trails, saddle and pack trips, scenic drives.

Santa Fe National Forest,
Santa Fe, New Mexico
Twenty-nine camp sites, 9 picnic sites, winter sports, wilderness pack trips, saddle trails

REGION 4
INTERMOUNTAIN REGION
Headquarters, Forest Service Building, Ogden, Utah

NATIONAL FORESTS
IN IDAHO

Boise National Forest,
Boise, Idaho
One hundred and twenty-one camp sites, twenty-two picnic sites, one swimming site, winter sports, scenic drives, primitive area at edge of Sawtooth.

Caribou National Forest,
Pocatello, Idaho
Sixteen camp sites, six picnic sites, winter sports, scenic drives, wilderness riding trails.

Challis National Forest,
Challis, Idaho
Primitive areas, nineteen camp

and picnic sites, scenic drive, riding and hiking trails, wilderness boating and pack trips. Commercial packers and guides.

Payette National Forest, McCall, Idaho

Primitive area, thirty-one camps and picnic sites, scenic drives and wilderness trips, winter sports.

Salmon National Forest, Salmon, Idaho

Primitive area, five camping sites, two picnic sites, forest roads, boat trips. (River of no return)

Sawtooth National Forest, Twin Falls, Idaho

Primitive areas, saddle and pack trips, scenic drives, fifty-seven camp sites, fifteen picnic sites, one swimming site, winter sports.

Targhee National Forest, St. Anthony, Idaho

Sixteen camp sites, seven picnic sites, riding and hiking trails, scenic drives, winter sports.

NATIONAL FORESTS IN NEVADA

Humboldt National Forest, Elko, Nevada

Wild areas, twenty-four camp sites, three picnic sites, saddle and pack trips, winter sports.

Toiyabe National Forest, Reno, Nevada

Wild areas, thirty-three camp and picnic sites, one swimming site, wilderness trips, wild areas, saddle and pack trips, scenic drives.

NATIONAL FORESTS IN UTAH

Ashley National Forest, Vernal, Utah

Primitive areas, thirty-three camp sites, three picnic sites, riding trails, wilderness pack trips, winter sports.

Cache National Forest, Logan, Utah

Forty-six camp sites, seventeen picnic sites, riding and hiking trails, winter sports, scenic drives.

Dixie National Forest, Cedar City, Utah

Thirteen camp sites, eight picnic sites, winter sports, wild areas.

Fishlake National Forest, Richfield, Utah

Twenty-four camp sites, five picnic sites, scenic drives.

Manti-La Sal National Forest, Price, Utah

Fifteen camp sites, four picnic sites, winter sports.

Uinta National Forest, Provo, Utah

Forty-two camp sites, six picnic sites, winter sports, scenic drive.

Wasatch National Forest, Salt Lake City, Utah

Fifty-one camp sites, twenty picnic sites, winter sports, boating, swimming, riding and hiking trails, wilderness trips, mountain climbing.

NATIONAL FORESTS IN WYOMING

Bridger National Forest,

Kemmerer, Wyoming

Twenty-four camp sites, two picnic sites, one swimming site, scenic drives, wilderness trips.

REGION 5
CALIFORNIA REGION

Headquarters, 630 Sansome St., San Francisco, California

NATIONAL FORESTS
IN CALIFORNIA

Angeles National Forest, Pasadena, California

Eighty-two camp sites, eleven picnic sites, two swimming sites, winter sports, scenic drives, riding and hiking trails, boating.

Cleveland National Forest, San Diego, California

Twenty-two camp sites, four picnic sites, primitive areas.

Eldorado National Forest, Placerville, California

Twenty-eight camp sites, three picnic sites, two swimming sites, winter sports, scenic drives, primitive areas, riding trails, wilderness trips.

Inyo National Forest, Bishop, California

Sixty-one camp sites, four picnic sites, two swimming sites, winter sports, wilderness trips.

Klamath National Forest, Yreka, California

Twenty-eight camp sites, two picnic sites, one swimming site, winter sports, hiking, riding, pack trips.

Lassen National Forest, Susanville, California

Fifty-nine camp sites, five picnic sites, one swimming site, winter sports, riding and hiking trails.

Los Padres National Forest, Santa Barbara, California

286 camp sites, seven picnic sites, scenic drives, ocean-side camping, wilderness trips, winter sports.

Mendocino National Forest, Willows, California

Forty-nine camp and picnic sites, saddle and pack trips, wilderness areas.

Modoc National Forest, Alturas, California

Twenty-five camp sites, two picnic sites, one swimming site, winter sports, scenic drive, wilderness trips.

Plumas National Forest, Quincy, California

Twenty-seven camp sites, two picnic sites, scenic drive.

San Bernadino National Forest, San Bernadino, California

Forty-one camp sites, ten picnic sites, camping and pack trips, two swimming sites, winter sports.

Sequoia National Forest, Porterville, California

Forty-five camp sites, eight picnic sites, eight swimming sites, winter sports, scenic drives, wilderness riding and hiking trails, boating.

Shasta-Trinity National Forest, Redding, California

Sixty-four camp sites, five picnic sites, eight swimming sites, winter sports, boating, primitive areas, wilderness areas, riding trails, scenic drives.

Sierra National Forest,
Fresno, California
Seventy-nine camp sites, nineteen picnic sites, twelve swimming sites, winter sports,
mountain climbing, pack and
saddle trips, boating.

Six Rivers National Forest,
Eureka, California
Thirty-three camp sites, one
picnic site, two swimming sites,
winter sports, riding trails,
scenic drives.

Stanislaus National Forest,
Sonora, California
Fifty-five camp and picnic
sites, two swimming sites, winter sports, scenic drives, saddle
and pack trips.

Tahoe National Forest,
Nevada City, California
Fifty-four camp sites, two picnic sites, three swimming sites,
winter sports, hiking and riding
trails, scenic drives.

REGION 6
PACIFIC NORTHWEST REGION
Headquarters, 729 N.E. Oregon
St., Portland 8, Oregon.

NATIONAL FORESTS
IN OREGON

Deschutes National Forests,
Bend, Oregon
Seventy-six camp sites, eleven
picnic sites, seven swimming
sites, winter sports, wild areas,
winderness areas, scenic drives,
saddle and pack trips.

Fremont National Forest,
Lakeview, Oregon
Twenty-one camp and picnic

sites, winter sports, wild areas.

Malheur National Forest,
John Day, Oregon
Thirty-nine camp and picnic
sites, winter sports, scenic
drives, saddle and pack trips.

Mount Hood National Forest,
Portland, Oregon
Wild areas, primitive areas,
swimming, saddle and pack
trips, winter sports.

Ochoco National Forest,
Prineville, Oregon
Twenty-eight camp and picnic
sites, scenic drives.

Rogue River National Forest,
Medford, Oregon
Forty-seven camp sites, three
picnic sites, one swimming site,
scenic drives, saddle and pack
trips, winter sports.

Siskiyou National Forest,
Grants Pass, Oregon
Eighteen camp sites, two picnic
sites, wild area, boat trips, saddle and pack trips, scenic
drives, pack outfitters.

Siuslaw National Forest,
Corvallis, Oregon
Twenty-three camp sites, four
picnic sites, swimming, boating, scuba diving, scenic drives.

Umatilla National Forest,
Pendleton, Oregon
Forty-four camp and picnic
sites, saddle and pack trips,
scenic drives, winter sports,
water sports.

Umpqua National Forest,
Roseburg, Oregon
Thirty-nine camp sites, one picnic site, four swimming sites,
scenic drives, saddle and pack
trips, winter sports.

Wallowa-Whitman National Forest,
Baker, Oregon

Forty camp sites, two picnic sites, wilderness areas, saddle and pack trips, scenic drives, water sports.

Willamette National Forest,
Eugene, Oregon

Sixty-nine camp and picnic sites, winter sports, scenic drives, saddle and pack trips.

Winema National Forest,
Klamath, Oregon

Wild area, scenic drives, camping and picnic facilities.

NATIONAL FORESTS IN WASHINGTON

Okanogan National Forest,
Okanogan, Washington

Fifty-two camp sites, one picnic site, two swimming sites, boating, saddle and pack trips, mountain climbing, winter sports.

Gifford Pinchot National Forest,
Vancouver, Washington

Fifty-four camp sites, two picnic sites, auto tours, saddle and pack trips, mountain climbing, winter sports, one swimming site.

Mount Baker National Forest,
Bellingham, Washington

Fifty-one camp sites, three picnic sites, winter sports, saddle and pack trips, mountain climbing.

Olympic National Forest,
Olympia, Washington

Fourteen camp sites, two picnic sites, two swimming sites, rain forests, saddle and pack trips, scenic drives.

Snoqualmie National Forest,
Seattle, Washington

One hundred camp and picnic sites, wild areas, scenic drives, saddle and pack trips, winter sports, outfitters available.

Wenatchee National Forest,
Wenatchee, Washington

Ninety-three camp sites, four picnic sites, winter sports, scenic drives, boat trips, saddle and pack trips.

REGION 7
EASTERN REGION
Headquarters, 6818 Market St., Upper Darby, Pennsylvania

NATIONAL FORESTS IN KENTUCKY

Cumberland National Forest,
Winchester, Kentucky

Four camp sites, eight picnic sites, swimming sites.

NATIONAL FORESTS IN NEW HAMPSHIRE

White Mountain National Forest,
Laconia, New Hampshire

Fourteen camp sites, six picnic sites, scenic drives, winter sports, rock climbing, swimming, foot trails.

NATIONAL FORESTS IN PENNSYLVANIA

Allegheny National Forest,
Warren, Pennsylvania

Seven camp sites, four picnic sites, scenic drives, three swimming sites, road-side tables.

NATIONAL FORESTS IN VERMONT

Green Mountain National Forest,

Rutland, Vermont
Eight camp sites, two picnic sites, swimming site, winter sports, scenic drives.

NATIONAL FORESTS IN VIRGINIA

George Washington National Forest,
Harrisonburg, Virginia
Nine camp sites, seven picnic sites, two swimming sites, scenic drives, foot trails.

Jefferson National Forest,
Roanoke, Virginia
Four camp sites, sixty picnic sites, two swimming sites.

NATIONAL FORESTS IN WEST VIRGINIA

Monongahela National Forest,
Elkins, West Virginia
Twenty-one camp sites, fifteen picnic sites, six swimming sites, horseback riding, scenic drives.

REGION 8
SOUTHERN REGION
Headquarters, 50 Seventh St., N.E. Atlanta 23, Georgia

NATIONAL FORESTS IN ALABAMA
(Supervisor's Address: 401 Federal Building, Montgomery, Alabama.)

William B. Bankhead National Forest
One camp site, three picnic sites, one swimming site.

Conecuh National Forest
One camping site, one picnic site, one swimming site.

Talladega National Forest
Four camping sites, seven picnic sites, one swimming site, scenic drive.

Tuskegee National Forest
Two picnic sites.

NATIONAL FORESTS IN ARKANSAS

Ouachita National Forest,
Hot Springs National Park,
Arkansas
Eight camp sites, seventeen picnic sites, eleven swimming sites, scenic drives, hiking.

Ozark National Forest,
Russellville, Arkansas
Ten camp and picnic sites, seven swimming sites, scenic drives.

NATIONAL FORESTS IN FLORIDA
(Supervisor's Address: 303 Petroleum Bldg., Tallahassee, Florida.)

Apalachicola National Forest
Four camp sites, ten picnic sites, four swimming sites, boating.

Ocala National Forest
Twelve camp sites, ten picnic sites, four swimming sites.

Osceola National Forest
One camp site, three picnic sites, two swimming sites, boating.

NATIONAL FORESTS IN GEORGIA

Chattahoochee National Forest,
Gainesville, Georgia
Ten camp sites, twenty-three picnic sites, six swimming sites, boating, hiking.

Oconee National Forest,
Gainesville, Georgia
Two picnic sites.

NATIONAL FORESTS IN LOUISIANA

Kisatchie National Forest, Alexandria, Louisiana
Two camp sites, six picnic sites, four swimming sites, boating, camping, scenic drives.

NATIONAL FORESTS IN MISSISSIPPI

(Supervisor's Address: P.O. Box 1144, Jackson, Mississippi.)

Bienville National Forest
Two camp sites, three picnic sites, one swimming site.

Delta National Forest
Camp sites, picnic sites.

DeSoto National Forest
Three camp sites, eight picnic sites, three swimming sites, boating.

Holly Springs National Forest
No improved recreation sites.

Homochitto National Forest
One camp site, three picnic sites, one swimming site.

Tombigbee National Forest
One camp site, two picnic sites, one swimming site, boating.

NATIONAL FORESTS IN NORTH CAROLINA

(Supervisor's Address: 42 N. French Broad Ave., Asheville, North Carolina.)

Croatan National Forest
Two picnic sites, two swimming sites, boating.

Nantahala National Forest
Ten camp sites, fifteen picnic sites, three swimming sites, hiking, boating, scenic drives.

Pisgah National Forest
Twenty-eight camping sites, twenty-three picnic sites, hiking, horse-back riding, swimming, scenic roads and trails.

Uwharrie National Forest
Recreational facilities not yet developed.

NATIONAL FORESTS IN SOUTH CAROLINA

(Supervisor's Address: 901 Sumter St., Columbia 1, South Carolina.)

Francis Marion National Forest
Three camp sites, ten picnic sites, boating.

Sumter National Forest
Two camp sites, twenty picnic sites, two swimming sites, scenic drives.

NATIONAL FORESTS IN TENNESSEE

Cherokee National Forest, Cleveland, Tennessee
Seventeen camp sites, twenty-seven picnic sites, nine swimming sites, hiking, boating.

NATIONAL FORESTS IN TEXAS

(Supervisor's Address: McFadden Bldg., P.O. Box 380, Lufkin, Texas.)

Angelina National Forest
Two camp sites, three picnic sites, one swimming site.

Davey Crockett National Forest
Two camp sites, three picnic sites, one swimming site.

Sabine National Forest
Two camp sites, three picnic sites, one swimming site.

Sam Houston National Forest
   Two camp sites, three picnic sites, one swimming site.

REGION 9
NORTH CENTRAL REGION
Headquarters 710 N. 6th St., Milwaukee 3, Wisconsin

NATIONAL FORESTS IN ILLINOIS

Shawnee National Forest,
Harrisburg, Illinois
   One camp site, twenty-four picnic sites, two swimming sites, boating.

NATIONAL FORESTS IN INDIANA

Hoosier National Forest,
Bedford, Indiana
   One camp site, two picnic sites, one swimming site, scenic drives.

NATIONAL FORESTS IN MICHIGAN

Ottawa National Forest,
Ironwood, Michigan
   Thirteen camp and picnic sites, 7 swimming sites, lake and stream fishing. Nearby winter sports areas.

Huron National Forest,
Cadillac, Michigan
   Lake Huron with magnificent beaches. 9 camp and picnic sites, trout fishing in famed Au Sable River, bird hunting, deer and small game.

Manistee National Forest,
Cadillac Michigan
   12 camp and picnic sites. Stream and lake fishing; deer and small game. Good skiing in northern sector.

Hiawatha National Forest,
Post Office Building,
Escanaba, Michigan
   Lakes: Michigan, Huron and Superior; lake and stream fishing for northern pike, walleye, bass, trout, perch; ruffed and sharptail groose shooting; deer and black bear hunting. 18 camp and picnic sites.

NATIONAL FORESTS IN MINNESOTA

Chippewa National Forest,
Cass Lake, Minnesota
   Twenty-one camp sites, thirty-three picnic sites, scenic drives, swimming, boating, winter sports.

Superior National Forest,
Duluth, Minnesota
   Twenty-nine camp sites, twelve picnic sites, canoeing, winter sports, scenic drives.

NATIONAL FORESTS IN MISSOURI

Clark National Forest,
Rolla, Missouri
   Three camp sites, six picnic sites, "John-boat float trips", river site camps.

Mark Twain National Forest,
Rolla, Missouri
   Eight camp sites, fourteen picnic sites, five swimming sites, scenic drives.

NATIONAL FORESTS IN OHIO

Wayne National Forest,
Bedford, Indiana
   One camp site, three picnic

sites, one swimming site, horse back riding, auto tours.

NATIONAL FORESTS IN WISCONSIN

Chequamegon National Forest, Park Falls, Wisconsin
Nine camp sites, fourteen picnic sites, winter sports, five swimming sites.

Nicolet National Forest, Rhinelander, Wisconsin
Nineteen camp sites, fourteen picnic sites, seven swimming sites, boating, canoe trips, snow shoeing and other winter sports.

REGION 10 ALASKA REGION

Headquarters, Federal and Territorial Bldg., P.O. Box 1631, Juneau, Alaska

NATIONAL FORESTS IN ALASKA

Chugach National Forest, Anchorage, Alaska
Five camp sites, sixteen picnic sites, one swimming site, winter sports, scenic trails and roads.

North Tongass National Forest, Juneau, Alaska
Five picnic sites, one swimming site, winter sports, boating, wilderness trails, mountain climbing.

South Tongass National Forest, Ketchikan, Alaska
Two camp sites, one picnic site, one swimming site.

NATIONAL FORESTS IN PUERTO RICO

Caribbean National Forest, Box AQ, Univ. Agr. Exp. Sta., Rio Piedras, Puerto Rico
(Write for complete details)

Now that we have all the information that one could imagine he might possibly need about our National Forests and National Parks would you believe that there is still a further list that will be of great value when you decide to make that trip. It is the following list of state agencies that will be sent you, on request. Information relating to travel within that state. Are you just taking your car? Will you be pulling a tent trailer or a deluxe trailer? No matter what you are driving or pulling behind that vehicle you will want to know what rules and regulations you will have to contend with in the various states that you will have to pass through to get to your destination. These agencies will also send you information concerning the places of interest in their states as well as information concerning game laws. But most important to you will be the travel information that will be relayed to you.

ALABAMA:
Dept. of Conservation, 711 High St., Montgomery 4, Alabama.

ALASKA:
Fish and Wildlife Service, Bureau of Sports Fisheries & Wildlife, Box 2021, Juneau, Alaska.

Div. of Econ. & Tour. Development, Dept. of National Resources, 310 Alaska Office Bldg., Juneau, Alaska.

ARIZONA:
Game and Fish Dept., 105 Arizona State Bldg., Phoenix, Arizona.
Development Board, 1521 W. Jefferson St., Phoenix, Arizona.

ARKANSAS:
Game and Fish Commission, Game and Fish Bldg., State Capitol Grounds, Little Rock, Arkansas.
Arkansas Pub. & Parks Comm., State Capitol Bldg., Little Rock, Arkansas.

CALIFORNIA:
Dept. of Fish & Game, 722 Capitol Ave., Sacramento 14, California.

Dept. of Natural Resources, Division of Beaches & Parks, P.O. Box 2390, Sacramento 11, California.

California State Cham. of Comm., 250 Bush Street, San Francisco 4, California.

All-Year Club of S. California, 628 W. 6th St., Los Angeles 17, California.

Redwood Empire Association, 46 Kearny St., San Francisco, California.

California Mission Trails Assn., 6912 Hollywood Blvd., Los Angeles 28, California.

Californians, Inc., 703 Market St., San Francisco, California.

Sierra Club, 1050 Mills Tower, San Francisco 4, California.

COLORADO:
Dept. of Game & Fish, 1530 Sherman St., Denver 3, Colorado.

Dept. of Public Relations, State Capitol, Denver 2, Colorado.

CONNECTICUT:
State Development Commission, State Office Bldg., Hartford 15, Connecticut.

DELAWARE:
Delaware State Development Dept., Dover, Delaware.

DISTRICT OF COLUMBIA:
Washington Con. & Vis. Bureau, 1616 K St., N.W., Washington 6, D.C.

National Parks Association, 1300 New Hampshire Ave. N.W., Washington 6, D.C.

National Capital Parks, Washington 25, D.C.

FLORIDA:
Game & Fresh Water Fish Commission, Tallahassee, Florida.

Tourist Services Div., Florida Devel. Comm., Carlton Bldg., East Wing, Tallahassee, Florida.

Florida Park Service, Tallahassee, Florida.

GEORGIA:
State Game & Fish Commission, 412 State Capitol, Atlanta, Georgia.

Georgia Dept. of Commerce, State Capitol, Atlanta, Georgia.

Dept. of State Parks, State Capitol, Atlanta 3, Georgia.

HAWAII:
Hawaii Visitors Bureau, 2051 Kalakaua Ave., Honolulu, Hawaii.

IDAHO:
Dept. of Fish & Game, 518 Front St., Boise, Idaho.

State Dept. of Comm. & Devel., Boise, Idaho.

ILLINOIS:
Dept. of Conservation, Division of Law Enforcement, 102 State Office Bldg., Springfield, Illinois.

Illinois Dept. Info. Service, 406 State Capitol, Springfield, Illinois.

INDIANA:
Dept. of Conservation, Division of Publicity, 311 W. Washington St., Indianapolis, Indiana. Dept. of Comm. & Pub. Rel., 333 State House, Indianapolis 4, Indiana.

IOWA:
State Conservation Commission, 7th and Court, Des Moines 9, Iowa.

Iowa Development Comm., 200 Jewett Bldg., Des Moines 9, Iowa

KANSAS:
Kansas Indus. Devel. Comm., State Office Bldg., Topeka, Kansas.

KENTUCKY:
Kentucky Dept. of Pub. Rel.,

New Capitol Annex, Frankfort, Kentucky.

Kentucky Tourist & Travel Commission, Room 66, Capitol Annex, Frankfort, Kentucky.

Dept. of Fish & Wildlife Resources, Frankfort, Kentucky.

LOUISIANA:
Wildlife & Fisheries Commission, 126 Civil Courts Bldg., New Orleans 16, Louisiana.

Dept. of Commerce & Industry, Tourist Bureau, P.O. Box 4291, Baton Rouge, Louisiana.

MAINE:
Dept. of Inland Fisheries & Game, State House, Augusta, Maine.

MARYLAND:
Director, Game & Inland Fish Commission, Annapolis, Maryland.

Department of Information, State Office Bldg., Annapolis, Maryland.

MASSACHUSETTS:
Division of Fisheries & Game, 73 Tremont St., Boston 8, Massachusetts.

Department of Commerce, 150 Causeway Street, Boston 14, Massachusetts.

MICHIGAN:
Michigan Tourist Council, Lansing 1, Michigan.

Dept. of Conservation, Lansing, Michigan.

MINNESOTA:
Div. of Promotion & Publ., Depart. of Business Development, 213 State Office Bldg., St. Paul 2, Minnesota.

State Parks Division, Conservation Department, State Office Building, St. Paul, Minnesota.

Division of Game & Fish, Room 337, State Office Bldg., St. Paul, Minnesota.

MISSISSIPPI:
Game & Fish Commission, P.O. Box 451, Jackson, Mississippi.

Mississippi Park Commission, 1104 Woolfolk State Office Bldg., Jackson, Mississippi.

Mississippi State Parks, P.O. Box 649, Jackson, Mississippi.

Mississippi Agric. & Indus. Bd., 1504 State Office Bldg., Jackson, Mississippi.

MISSOURI:
Missouri Div. of Res. & Devel., State Office Bldg., Jefferson City, Missouri.

MONTANA:
I. & E. Division, Montana State Fish and Game Dept., Helena, Montana.

State Highway Commission, Helena, Montana.

Advertising Director, Montana State High. Comm., Helena, Montana.

NEBRASKA:
Nebraska Game, Forestation & Parks Commission, State Capitol, 9th Floor, Lincoln 9, Nebraska.

NEVADA:
Nevada Dept. of Econ. Devel., Capitol Building, Carson City, Nevada.

Fish & Game Commission, Box 678, Reno, Nevada.

NEW HAMPSHIRE:
Fish & Game Dept., 34 Bridge St., Concord, New Hampshire.

New Hampshire State Plan. & Devel. Comm., Concord, New Hampshire.

NEW JERSEY:
Division of Fish & Game, 230 W. State St., Trenton 25, New Jersey.

Div. of Planning & Devel., Dept. of Conservation & Economic Development, 520 E. State St., Trenton, New Jersey.

National Campers & Hikers Assn. Inc., Box 451, Orange, New Jersey.

NEW MEXICO:
Dept. of Game & Fish, Box 2060, Santa Fe, New Mexico.

New Mexico Dept. of Devel., P.O. Box 1716, Santa Fe, New Mexico.

NEW YORK:
State Dept. of Commerce, 112 State St., Albany, New York.

Camping Council, Inc., 17 East 48th Street, N.Y. 17, New York.

NORTH CAROLINA:
Wildlife Resources Commission, Box 2919, Raleigh, North Carolina.

Advertising Division, Dept. of Conservation & Development, Raleigh, North Carolina.

NORTH DAKOTA:

State Game & Fish Dept., Capitol Bldg., Bismarck, North Dakota.

N.D. State Highway Comm., Bismarck, North Dakota.

State Historical Society, Bismarck, North Dakota.

OHIO:
Dept. of National Resources, 1500 Dublin Rd., Columbus 12, Ohio.

Ohio Develop. & Pub. Comm., 21 W. Broad St., Columbus 15, Ohio.

OKLAHOMA:
Dept. of Wildlife Conservation, Oklahoma City 5, Oklahoma.

Div. of Publ. & Tour. Information, Oklahoma Plan. & Res. Board, 533 State Capitol, Oklahoma City 5, Oklahoma.

OREGON:
State Game Commission, 1634 S.W. Alder, Portland 8, Oregon.

Travel Information Division, State Highway Dept., Salem, Oregon.

PENNSYLVANIA:
State Dept. of Forests & Waters, Harrisburg, Pennsylvania.

Bureau of Travel Devel., Pennsylvania Dept. of Comm., 129 Capitol Bldg., Harrisburg, Pennsylvania.

RHODE ISLAND:
Division of Fish & Game, Veteran's Memorial Bldg., 83 Park Street, Providence, Rhode Island.

Information Division, Development Council, State House, Providence 3, Rhode Island.

Publicity & Recreation Div., Rhode Island Devel. Council, Roger Williams Building, Providence 8, Rhode Island.

SOUTH CAROLINA:
South Carolina Devel. Board, Columbia, South Carolina.

Director, Wildlife Resources Dept., Division of Game, Box 360, Columbia, South Carolina.

SOUTH DAKOTA:
Dept. of Game, Fish & Parks, Pierre, South Dakota.

Publicity Director, State Highway Comm., Pierre, South Dakota.

TENNESSEE:
Div. of State Information, Dept. of Conservation, Nashville, Tennessee.

Game & Fish Commission, I. & E. Section, Cordell Hull Bldg., 6th Ave. N., Nashville, Tennessee.

Division of State Parks, 203 Cordell Hull Bldg., Nashville, Tennessee.

TEXAS:
Information Service, Texas Hwy. Dept., Austin, Texas.

State Parks Board, Drawer E., Capitol Station, Austin, Texas.

Game & Fish Commission, Director of Law Enforcement, Walton Bldg., Austin 14,

Texas.

UTAH:
Utah Tour. & Pub. Council, 327 State Capitol Bldg., Salt Lake City, Utah.

Dept. of Fish & Game, 1596 West North Temple, Salt Lake City, Utah.

Tourist & Publicity Council, 327 State Capitol Bldg., Salt Lake City, Utah.

VERMONT:
Vermont Devel. Comm., Montpelier, Vermont.

Department of Forest & Parks, Montpelier, Vermont.

VIRGINIA:
Div. of Public Rel. & Adv., Virginia Dept. of Con. & Dev., 315 State Office Bldg., Richmond, Virginia.

Division of Parks, Conservation Commission, Richmond 19, Virginia.

WASHINGTON:
Wash. State Dept. of Comm., State Capitol, Olympia, Washington.

Dept. of Game, 600 N. Capitol Way, Olympia, Washington.

State Resort Assn., 2100 Fifth Ave., Seattle, Washington.

Tourist Promotion Division, Department of Commerce and Economic Dev., General Administration Bldg., Olympia, Washington.

WEST VIRGINIA:
W. Va. Indus. & Pub. Comm., State Capitol, Charleston 5, West Virginia.

Conservation Commission, Div. of Education, Room 663, State Office Bldg., Charleston, West Virginia.

WISCONSIN:
Recreational Pub. Section, Wisconsin Conserv. Dept., 830 State Office Bldg., Madison, Wisconsin.

Conservation Department, P.O. Box 450, Madison 1, Wisconsin.

WYOMING:
Wyoming Travel Commission, Capitol Bldg., Cheyenne, Wyoming.

Game & Fish Commission, Box 378, Cheyenne, Wyoming.

PUERTO RICO:
Puerto Rico Visitors Bureau, San Juan, Puerto Rico.

Puerto Rico Visitors Bureau, 666 Fifth Avenue, New York, New York.

VIRGIN ISLANDS:
Tourist Development Board, St. Thomas, Virgin Islands.

Virgin Islands National Park, P.O. Box 1589, Charlotte Amalie, St. Thomas, Virgin Islands.

Our good neighbors north of the border and south of the border welcome United States citizens to the camping grounds in their countries. A request from you will bring many brochures which you will want to frame. ●